R 746.92 S817w   F V
STEGEMEYER
 WHO'S WHO IN FASHION
                                13.50

WITHDRAWN

St. Louis Community College

Library

5801 Wilson Avenue
St. Louis, Missouri 63110

WHO'S WHO
IN FASHION

ANNE STEGEMEYER

WHO'S WHO IN FASHION

Fairchild Publications
New York

To the memory of
Josephine Ellis Watkins
who saw a need and filled it

Contents

Preface _____

Josephine Ellis Watkins was teaching at the Fashion Institute of Technology when she realized there was no source from which her students could gain "an awareness of the contribution of individuals to the field of fashion." She immediately moved to compile information to fill the void and this book, *Who's Who in Fashion* is a direct descendant of her original inspiration.

Rewarding though it may be, the fashion business is difficult, demanding and volatile with a constantly changing cast of characters. Talents appear, star for a while and drop out of sight, pop into view again. Others produce successfully and consistently year after year. Recording this scene is a continuing process, never finished, always incomplete. The emphasis here is on today's established designers, with a brief survey of influential figures in related fields and of the past.

In *Who's Who in Fashion,* I've tried to give some sense of the excitement of the world of fashion, the diversity of the people who've made their careers in it, the differences in their approaches to the business of clothing people and in the paths that led them to success. I hope the book will be useful to students and professionals, and to people everywhere who love clothes and share my fascination with this extraordinary business.

Anne Stegemeyer
New York City

1980

Designed by Elaine Golt Gongora

Acknowledgments _____

Information for the *Who's Who in Fashion* biographies was culled from questionnaires, press clippings, published biographies and personal interviews. Writers working away at their own specialities have also been generous with facts not otherwise readily available.

My sincere thanks to all: Ellin Saltzman of Saks Fifth Avenue for her advice in the planning stages; Merle Thomason of the *Women's Wear Daily* Library, untiring in her search for the definitive interview, the corroborative detail, the authentic date; Betty Kirke for her help on Vionnet; Gordon Stone at the Metropolitan Museum Costume Library, unfailing in his courtesy. Thanks, too, to my diligent editor, Olga Kontzias, and to Ed Gold, patient and understanding publisher.

Most especially, Annalee Gold has my deepest gratitude for her support during those dark hours when I *knew* the book would never get done. Without her telephone therapy sessions it might very well not have.

NAMES TO KNOW

Adrian, Gilbert
Antonelli, Maria
Balenciaga, Cristobal
Banton, Travis
Beaton, Cecil
Bertin, Rose
Brigance, Tom
Callot Soeurs
Carnegie, Hattie
Carven
Chanel, Gabrielle "Coco"
Chase, Edna Woolman
Connolly, Sybil
Creed, Charles
Daché, Lilly
Daves, Jessica
de Rauch, Madeleine
Dessès, Jean
Dior, Christian
Erté
Fairchild, John
Fath, Jacques
Ferragamo, Salvatore
Fogarty, Anne
Fontana

Fortuny, Mariano
Hartnell, Norman
James, Charles
Klein, Anne
Lanvin, Jeanne
Lelong, Lucien
Mainbocher
McCardell, Claire
Molyneux, Captain Edward
Norell, Norman
Paquin, House of
Partos, Emeric "Imre"
Patou, Jean
Pedlar, Sylvia
Piguet, Robert
Poiret, Paul
Pope, Virginia
Quant, Mary
Ricci, Nina
Rochas, Marcel
Schiaparelli, Elsa
Snow, Carmel
Vionnet, Madeleine
Vreeland, Diana
Worth, Charles Frederick

Adrian, Gilbert
(born Adrian Adolph Greenburg)

(American designer)

BORN: Naugatuck, Connecticut, March 1903.

DIED: Los Angeles, California, 13 September 1959.

AWARDS:
1943—Neiman-Marcus Award
1945—Coty American Fashion Critics' "Winnie"
1956—Parsons Medal for Distinguished Achievement

1946

Top Hollywood designer in 20s and 30s. Attended School of Fine and Applied Arts in New York, 1921; went to Paris to study in 1922 where he met Irving Berlin. Designed for *Music Box Revues,* Greenwich Village *Follies,* and George White's *Scandals.*

Adrian's costumes caught the eye of Natacha Rambova who wanted him to design costumes for her husband, Rudolph Valentino; went to Hollywood in 1923. In 1925 began association with Metro-Goldwyn-Mayer which lasted until 1939. As chief designer he created costumes for Joan Crawford, Greta Garbo, Katherine Hepburn, Rosalind Russell, Norma Shearer, among others. Married to actress Janet Gaynor; one son, Robin.

Opened his own business, Adrian Ltd., in Beverly Hills for both made-to-order and top bracket ready-to-wear, 1941. Designed stage costumes for Billie Burke and Ilka Chase, 1944. Produced several men's wear collections; two perfumes, "Saint" and "Sinner." Closed retail salon, 1948; made African safari, 1949; continued in wholesale until 1953. Retired to Brazil with his wife where he concentrated on landscape painting, a longtime avocation. Returned to Hollywood, 1958. In 1959, at the time of his death, he was working on costumes for the 1960 stage production of *Camelot.*

Adrian's style was marked by dramatic shoulder interest—exaggeratedly wide, padded shoulders tapering to a small waist. Not surprisingly, he strongly opposed the sloping shoulders DIOR introduced in 1947. Signature details were diagonal closings, dolman sleeves, floating tabs. He was influenced by African wildlife, modern art and that of ancient Egypt, using set-in patches of color, dramatic animal prints on sinuous black crepe evening gowns. He worked stripes in opposing directions; mixed gingham checks in different sizes, sometimes quilted and sequined. In general, his look was sleek and modern but he also did draped, swathed late-day dresses, and romantic organdy evening gowns. One of these, the "Letty Lynton" gown designed for Joan Crawford, was an enormous popular success and widely copied, reputedly more than 500,000 sold at Macy's alone.

Antonelli, Maria

(Italian couturière and fashion pioneer)

BORN: 1903.
DIED: 1969.

Began as dressmaker in 1924; important for coats and suits from 1930s through 1960s. Started Antonelli-Sport in 1933 assisted by daughter Luciana, who trained with her. Employed ANDRÉ LAUG and Guy Douvier, both to become successful designers on their own. Was one of first to participate in Florence showings of February 1951.

Balenciaga, Cristobal

(Spanish-French couturier)

BORN: Guetaria, Spain, 21 January 1895.
DIED: Valencia, Spain, 24 March 1972.

Balenciaga's father is said to have been captain of the Spanish royal yacht (or a fishing boat captain) and died when Cristobal was 13. The boy and his mother moved to San Sebastián, where she became a seamstress. Little is known of his childhood and education but he is said to have been devoted to his mother, learning her craft and becoming a skilled tailor. According to legend, his career began at 13 when the

1943

1945

1937

1939

1944

1941

1938

1942

1946

Drawn by Balenciaga's sketchers and approved by him

4

Marquesa de Casa Torres allowed him to copy a Dré-coll suit of hers. She encouraged him to leave home to study design and in 1916 helped him to set up his own shop in San Sebastián. This was the first of three houses called "Eisa"; the others were established in Madrid in 1932 and Barcelona in 1928. Moved to Paris in 1937, opening a shop on avenue George V; his reputation grew rapidly and he soon was regarded as one of the most imaginative and creative artists of the Paris couture.

Balenciaga loathed publicity, never appeared in his own salon, was seldom photographed, and, except for his perfumes, refused to have anything to do with commercial exploitation. A perfectionist tailor, he was the only couturier who could design, cut, sew, and fit an entire garment; he was revered by his staff as the "Master." GIVENCHY, COURRÈGES, and UNGARO were among his disciples. He refused to compromise with the "yeh-yeh" fashion of the 1960s; retired and closed house, 1968. Came out of retirement to design wedding dress for marriage of Carmencita de Martinez Bordiu, granddaughter of Generalissimo Franco, to

1947

1947

1950

1950

1952

1953

1954

1955

1956

Prince Alfonso de Borbon, which took place in 1972, two weeks before Balenciaga died at age 77.

He was a great student of art and understood the interpretive use of source material. The influence of the old Spanish masters, whose somber blacks and browns were among his favorite colors, and of such early moderns as Monet and Manet, can be traced in his work. His innovations, especially during the 1950s, are still influential. Among them: revolutionary semi-fitted jacket, 1951; the middy dress which evolved into the chemise, 1955; cocoon coat; balloon skirt; flamenco evening gown with skirt cut long in back, short in front. As this is being written, one is still struck by the architectural quality of Balenciaga's designs and by their essential "rightness," and impressed by the mastery of the hand and eye that created them. He is rightly considered one of the giants of twentieth-century couture.

Balenciaga in 1967

1957

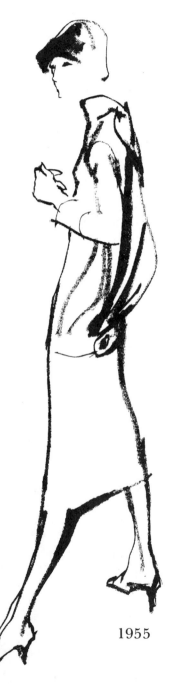

1955

Banton, Travis _____

(American film designer)

BORN: Waco, Texas, 1874.
DIED: 1958.

In New York attended Columbia University, Art Student's League, School of Fine and Applied Arts. First employed as designer by Madame Frances; in 1924, at instigation of Walter Wanger, went to Hollywood to design gowns for Leatrice Joy in Paramount Pictures' *The Dressmaker from Paris.** Stayed on and in the 1930s became head designer at Paramount.

At expiration of contract in 1938 went to 20th Century Fox; worked off and on for Universal Studios; in the 1950s turned to designing ready-to-wear. In 1956 designed Rosalind Russell's wardrobe for the stage production *Auntie Mame;* did clothes for Dinah Shore's personal and television appearances.

Banton had an extraordinarily long career, is remembered particularly for what became known as "the Paramount look." He produced clothes of the highest quality, superb in fabrics, workmanship and fit, often cut on the bias, dreamy, elegant and understated.

*This title also given as *A Dressmaker of Paris* and *A Dressmaker in Paris.*

Beaton, Cecil _____
(Sir Cecil Walter Hardy Beaton)

(English photographer, artist,
costume and set designer)

BORN: London, England,
14 January 1904.

AWARDS:
Antoinette Perry Award:
1955—*Quadrille*
1957—*My Fair Lady*
1970—*Coco*
1956—Neiman-Marcus
Award
1957—C.B.E.
Motion Picture Academy
Award:
1958—*Gigi*
1965—*My Fair Lady* (sets
and costumes)

Educated at Harrow and Cambridge University. Knighted, 1972.

In 1928, began a long association with *Vogue,* first contributing fragile, spidery sketches, caricatures of well-known London actresses and drawings of clothes worn at society parties, later photography. In her memoirs,* EDNA WOOLMAN CHASE of *Vogue* described him at their first meeting: ". . . tall, slender, swaying like a reed, blond, and very young . . ." His aura was "an odd combination of airiness and assurance." And later: "What I like best is his debunking attitude toward life and his ability for hard work."

In photography he did both fashion and portraits; became the favored photographer of the British royal

*Edna Woolman Chase and Ilka Chase, *Always in Vogue* (New York, 1966), pp. 212–213.

1960—French Legion
of Honor

PUBLICATIONS:
The Book of Beauty. London:
Duckworth, 1930.
Cecil Beaton's New York.
London: Batsford, 1938.
Persona Grata (with Kenneth
Tynan). London: Wingate,
1953.
The Glass of Fashion. London:
Weidenfeld & Nicolson,
1954.
*Cecil Beaton's Diaries—
1922–1929, The Wandering
Years* (1961); *1939–1944,
The Years Between* (1965);
*1944–1948, The Happy
Years* (1972); *1948–1955,
The Strenuous Years* (1973).
London: Weidenfeld &
Nicolson.
The Gainsborough Girls, a play.
1951.

family; photographed during World War II for the wartime Ministry of Information, traveling widely to North Africa, Burma, and China.

Beginning in 1935, Beaton designed scenery and costumes for ballet, opera, and many theatrical productions in both London and New York. Credits include: *Lady Windermere's Fan, Quadrille, The Grass Harp, The School for Scandal* (Comédie Française); costumes for *My Fair Lady,* New York and London productions; *Coco.* Film credits include: *Gigi, The Doctor's Dilemma, My Fair Lady.*

Prolific writer, approximately twenty-eight books of his own as well as illustrator with photographs and drawings of many others.

Beaton lives in England. For recreation devotes himself to diaries, scrapbooks, decoration, and travel.

Bertin, Rose
(born Marie Jeanne Laurent Bertin)

*(French milliner and dressmaker to
Marie Antoinette)*

BORN: near Abbeville, France,
2 July 1747.
DIED: Epinay, France,
22 September 1813.

Came to Paris at 16 as apprentice in millinery shop run by Mlle. Pagelle; sent to deliver hats to royal princesses at Hotel de Conti where she was noticed by the Princesse de Conti, who became her sponsor. Bertin taken on as partner in shop. Appointed court milliner in 1772; introduced to Marie Antoinette and became her close confidante.

Her establishment, "Au Grand-Mogol," became extremely successful, not only with the French court but with the diplomatic corps, executing commissions for dresses and hats to be sent to foreign courts. Thus she was one of the early exporters of French fashion. She also produced fantastic headdresses reflecting current events, creations which were enormously costly and symbolic of the excesses that led to the French Revolution.

Bertin could be considered the first "name" designer, celebrated and mentioned in contemporary

Marie Antoinette, patroness of Rose Bertin

memoirs and encyclopedias. She was proud, arrogant, ambitious, and so influential she was dubbed "The Minister of Fashion." She remained loyal to the Queen until her death; fled to England, returning in 1800 to eke out her last years selling trinkets; died in poverty.

To quote from an obituary written at her death: "Mlle. Bertin is justly famous for the supremacy to which she has raised French fashions and for her services to the industries that made the material she used in her own creations and those that she inspired others to make."

Brigance, Tom

(American designer)

BORN: Waco, Texas,
4 February 1913.

AWARDS:
1953—Coty American
Fashion Critics' "Winnie"
International Silk Citation
National Cotton Award

Son of English mother, French father. Attended Waco Junior College in Texas; Parsons School of Design and National Academy of Art in New York; pursued studies further in Paris. Returned to New York where his talent was recognized by Dorothy Shaver; in 1939 he became Lord & Taylor's exclusive designer. Spent 1941 to 1944 in Air Corps Intelligence; decorated for leadership and bravery. Returned to Lord & Taylor, 1944; went to work on Seventh Avenue, 1949.

During his years on Seventh Avenue he designed everything from coats and suits to day and evening dresses, beachwear, blouses and play clothes. Specialized in beachwear for many years and is well known for the swimsuits he designed for Sinclair, treasured by women for flattering cut and excellent fit. He was among the first to use over-sized patterns, geometrics, large florals, and to mix patterns such as checks and stripes.

Brigance lives in New York City, summers on Long Island; collects books and Regency furniture; is an ardent and gifted gardener. He has lectured extensively on fashion in major cities of the United States.

Callot Soeurs

(French couture house)

French couture house founded 1895 by three sisters, daughters of an antique dealer (or painter). All were talented but it was the eldest, Mme. Gerber, who was the genius. Tall, gaunt, her hair dyed a brilliant red, she was usually dressed in a baglike costume covered with oriental jewelry and ropes of fresh water pearls. Her two sisters eventually retired and she became the sole proprietor of the house, which at one time had branches in London and New York.

Mme. Gerber was a dressmaker of great technical skill and also an artist of impeccable taste—an originator. She created the first draped skirt drawn up in front, did remarkable things with the kimono sleeve, and had a flair for exquisite embroidery. The second sister, Mme. Vertran, is given credit for the first draped evening dress fastened at the belt with an artificial rose. It was, however, the high standard of excellence maintained in collection after collection over a period of many years which built the Callot reputation.

The house was noted for color richness, intricate cut and, particularly, for formal evening wear. It was famous for delicate lace blouses, the use of gold and silver lamé, chiffon, georgette, organdy, rococo flower embroidery, and embroidery in Chinese colors. The noted Spanish-American beauty, Mrs. Rita de Acosta Lydig, was a client and was rumored to have provided financial backing.

Henri Bendel was a great admirer of Mme. Gerber, referring to her as the backbone of the fashion world of Europe. She was an early influence on MADELEINE VIONNET, who spent some time at Callot.

During the 1920s Callot produced every up-to-the-minute look—dresses, lounging pajamas, evening dresses with layered tulle skirts embellished with silk roses, pleated skirt and middy top outfits—always with such taste, subtlety, and superb workmanship that the clothes had the timelessness and elegance of classics. The most fashionable women of the world went there to dress.

The house closed in 1953.

1931

Carnegie, Hattie
(born Henrietta Kanengeiser)

(American designer and manufacturer)

BORN: Vienna, Austria, 1886.
DIED: New York City,
  22 February 1956.

AWARDS:
  1939—Neiman-Marcus
    Award
  1948—Coty American
    Fashion Critics' "Winnie"

Changed name to Carnegie in emulation of "richest man in the world," Andrew Carnegie. Married briefly in 1918, again in 1922. In 1928 married Major John Zanft, who survived her. No children.

In early teens answered ad to pin hats in millinery workroom; worked for several milliners, as messenger girl at Macy's, as millinery model; in the late night hours designed hats for neighborhood women. She did not sew then and never learned. In 1909 opened "Carnegie-Ladies Hatter" on East Tenth Street, New York. In 1915, with Rose Roth, a seamstress, opened custom dressmaking salon on West 86th Street off Broadway, near fashionable Riverside Drive. Roth made dresses, Carnegie made hats and waited on customers, who hoped the clothes would make them look like Hattie Carnegie. Carnegie bought out her partner two years later.

She made her first buying trip to Europe in 1919, from then on went four times a year, bringing back quantities of Paris models; major part of business still done with her own designs. Bought building at 42 East 49th Street in 1925; expanded over the years into multi-million dollar business, including two resort shops, made-to-order workrooms, ready-to-wear factories, millinery, jewelry, perfumes. Said to have been first American designer to put name on a ready-to-wear label. She dressed society beauties, movie and stage stars such as Constance Bennett, Tallulah Bankhead and Joan Crawford. In early 1930s was forced to recognize hard facts of depression, opened a ready-to-wear department in her shop where a good VIONNET copy could be had for as little as $50. In 1934, established Spectator Sports, a wholesale firm, which was extremely successful.

Carnegie was tiny, less than five feet tall, very feminine, a shrewd businesswoman, but above all she loved clothes. She employed three assistant designers, two sketchers, and her knack for discovering design talent was legendary. At different times, NORMAN NORELL, PAULINE TRIGÈRE and CLAIRE McCARDELL all worked for her. Her designs were youthful and sophisticated, never faddy, never extreme, eternally Carnegie no matter what the trends might be. She was noted for "little" suits with nipped waists and rounded hips, especially becoming to smaller women; embroidered, beaded evening suits; at-home pajamas; long wool dinner dresses and theater suits. Beautiful fabrics and excellent workmanship were hallmarks; anything but the best was abhorrent to her. Her clothing business continued for some years after her death.

Carven (Madame Carven Mallet)

(French couturière)

Daughter of Italian father, French mother. Planned to study architecture and archaeology, was diverted into dressmaking by her tiny size which made it difficult to find clothes.

Opened couture house in 1944, with backing of decorator husband, specializing in imaginative sports, beach and dress-up clothes for petite young women like herself; emphasis on small waists and rounded hips. Collaborated with accessory designers to find handbags, shoes, hats, in proportion to the small figure. Successful perfume, "Ma Griffe." House still open in late 1970s.

Chanel, Gabrielle "Coco"

(French couturière)

BORN: Saumur, France, 19 August 1883.
DIED: Paris, France, 10 January 1971.

AWARDS:
1957—Neiman-Marcus Award

On her mother's death, she was sent at age 6 to live with paternal grandmother in Moulins.

In 1910 started making hats in a Paris apartment. Opened shop in Deauville. Moved Paris workshop to 14, rue Cambon. In 1914 made first dresses using wool jersey, a material not at that time utilized in French fashion, often trimmed with rabbit fur.

By 1919 she was famous. Slender, vital, with a low, warm voice, a superb saleswoman. Couture house now at 25, rue Cambon, later enlarged to include 27, 29, 31. While not relevant to her design ability, her personality and private life contributed to her success. Through Misia and José María Sert she met and associated with leading figures in the art world of the 1920s: Diaghilev, Picasso, Cocteau, dancer Serge

1957   1958   1960

1929

Lifar, decorator-designer Léon Bakst. While she never married, there were many love affairs. Grand Duke Dmitri, grandson of Czar Alexander II, was a frequent escort; she maintained a three-year liaison with the Duke of Westminster.

In addition to couture, Chanel's empire encompassed perfumes, a costume jewelry workshop and for a time, a textile house. "Chanel No. 5" was created, 1922; Parfums Chanel was established to market perfumes, 1924; by 1935, in addition to No. 5, there were "Bois des Iles," "Chanel No. 22," "Cuir de Russie." Other perfumes and a line of cosmetics have been introduced since her death.

Chanel closed couture house September 1939, at outset of World War II. In 1953, aged 70, she decided to go back into business, thinking first of a mass-production arrangement with an American manufacturer. Instead, her first postwar collection was presented 5 February 1954, six months before her seventy-first birthday. A continuation of her original themes of simplicity and wearability, it was not well received by the Paris press but was bought heavily by American stores and found instant acceptance among American women. Success followed in France, continuing into the 1960s when her refusal to change basic style or raise hemlines led to a decline in her influence and her business. Within a few years, the pendulum swung back and she was vindicated.

In 1969 her life was the basis for *Coco,* a Broadway musical starring Katherine Hepburn.

Chanel, "La Grande Mademoiselle," died on a Sunday night in January 1971, working to the last on a new collection. The House of Chanel has continued, directed in succession by Gaston Berthelot, Ramon Esparza, long-time assistant to Balenciaga, and since 1975, by Jean Cazubon and Yvonne Dudel who originally trained under Chanel. Ready-to-wear was added in the fall of 1977, with PHILIPPE GUIBOURGÉ as designer.

In evaluating Chanel, some place her alongside such giants as VIONNET and BALENCIAGA, others see her as more personality than creator, with an innate knack for knowing what women would want a few seconds before they knew it themselves. Certainly her early designs exerted a liberating influence and even the evening clothes had a youthful quality that was all her own. Her daytime palette was neutral—black,

Chanel with Sam Goldwyn, 1931

white, beige, red—with pastels introduced at night. Trademarks were the little-boy look, wool jersey dresses with white collars and cuffs, pea jackets, bell-bottom trousers. Personal touches were bobbed hair, suntanned skin, magnificent jewelry worn with sportswear.

In her second period she is best remembered for her suits, made of jersey or the finest, softest Scottish tweeds. Jackets were usually collarless and trimmed with braid, blouses soft and tied at the neckline, skirts at or just below the knee. Suits were shown with multiple strands of pearls and gold chains set with enormous fake stones; in her own case mixed with real jewels. Other signatures were quilted handbags with shoulder chains, beige sling-back pumps with black tips, flat black hairbows, a single gardenia. She remains a legend for her taste and wit and personal style, for her unfaltering dedication to perfection and a luxury based on the most refined simplicity of cut, superb materials, and workmanship of the highest order.

Chase, Edna Woolman _____
(born Edna Woolman Alloway)

(Fashion editor)

BORN: Asbury Park,
   New Jersey, 1877.
DIED: 1957.

AWARDS:
   1935—French Legion of
      Honor
   1940—Neiman-Marcus
      Award
PUBLICATIONS:
   Chase, Edna Woolman and
      Ilka Chase. *Always in Vogue.*
      Garden City, New York:
      Doubleday & Co., Inc.,
      1954.

Parents divorced; Edna raised by Quaker grandparents; took stepfather's name, Martin, when mother remarried. Married and divorced Francis Dane Chase; one child, actress, writer Ilka Chase. Married in 1921 to Richard Newton, who died in 1950.

In 1895, at age 18, she went to work in the Circulation Department at *Vogue,* which was then just two years old. Her duties were to add new names to the subscription list, address envelopes in which subscription forms were sent out. Salary, $10 a week. She was to spend fifty-six years on the magazine, thirty-seven years as editor.

She fell in love with the magazine immediately and as she was eager, enthusiastic, hard working, willing to take on any and all chores, acquired more and more responsibility. By 1911 she was the equivalent of managing editor; her name first appeared as editor on the masthead in February 1914. British *Vogue* was born in 1916; French *Vogue*'s first issue was June 1920. Mrs. Chase was editor-in-chief of all three editions. During her tenure *Vogue* survived two world wars, a depression, tremendous social changes. With Condé Nast, who acquired it in 1909, she helped shape it according to her own strong sense of propriety, her high standards of professionalism. She suffered the second-rate badly, respected talent and hard work, wrote directly to the point.

She is credited with originating the modern fashion show in 1914 when Vogue produced a benefit "Fashion Fête" sponsored by prominent society women, presenting the creations of the best New York houses. During World War I she also began to feature American designers in *Vogue*'s pages. Taste, business ability and a capacity for hard work brought her to the top of her profession and kept her there for an amazing span. She retired as editor-in-chief in 1952 and became chairman of the editorial board.

Her advice to those thinking of a career in fashion, although written in the early 1950s is still worth considering. Requirements for success were taste, sound judgment, and experience, that training and knowledge gained from the slow process of actually working in a business. She valued this kind of learning above course-taking which, in a gardener's term, she described as "top dressing," not much good without the subsoil of a real apprenticeship.

Connolly, Sybil

(Irish designer)

BORN: Swansea, Wales,
    c. 1921.

On her father's death when she was 15, Sybil moved with her mother and two sisters to Waterford in southern Ireland. In 1938 went to work for Bradley's, a London dressmaker, where she stayed for two years of pin holding. Applied for and got job as buyer at Richard Alan, Dublin specialty shop, went on to become a director of the company, building the store's couture department into a thriving business. When the store's designer left in 1950, Connolly designed a small collection which sold very well and was the start of her design career.

Discovered in early 1950s by CARMEL SNOW of *Harper's Bazaar* and by The Fashion Group of Philadelphia on a visit to Dublin. In 1953 she took a collection to the United States where her one-of-a-kind designs and beautiful Irish fabrics made a strong and favorable impression. Left Richard Alan in 1957 to set up her own firm, Sybil Connolly, Inc., with a special boutique for ready-to-wear. Clothes were carried by fine specialty stores across the United States. In the 1970s she has brought custom collections to New York, showing them in a friend's Fifth Avenue apartment, taking orders to be made up in her Dublin shop.

Connolly is known for her use of iridescent Donegal tweeds; evening dresses with ruffled tops; skirts made of handkerchief linen worked in horizontal mushroom pleats; crocheted lace and Carrickmacross lace; Connemars shawls used for daytime dresses. Her clothes are simple in cut, extremely wearable, notable for fabric and workmanship.

Creed, Charles

(English couturier)

BORN: Paris, France, 1908.
DIED: London, England, July 1966.

PUBLICATIONS:
Maid to Measure. London: Jarrolds, 1961.

Descendant of long line of English tailors. House first established as men's tailors in London, 1710. Charles's grandfather, Henry, opened a Paris establishment, 1850, established reputation for finest tailored riding habits for women in Europe. Clients included actress Réjane, Empress Eugénie of France, England's Queen Victoria, opera singer Mary Garden, the spy Mata Hari. Under the direction of Henry's son, the house expanded into tailored suits and sports clothes, even evening dresses.

Creed studied in France, Berlin, Vienna, Scotland, United States; entered family business in Paris, 1930. Opened his own London house, first showing in 1932; closed Paris business a few years later. Married in 1948 to Patricia Cunningham, fashion editor of British *Vogue,* who went to work for him in 1963. Designed a wholesale line for Eric Hill of London in 1950s; opened a boutique in 1955; in 1956 did a line for David Crystal produced under the Creed label. Closed couture house in March 1966 to concentrate on ready-to-wear subsidiary.

Creed was distinguished for sound traditional tailoring and excellent fabrics; elegant suits for town, country, evening; bright printed blouses of sheer Rodier wool.

Daché, Lilly

(French-born American milliner)

BORN: Beigles, France.

AWARDS:
   1940—Neiman-Marcus
   Award
   1943—Coty American
   Fashion Critics' Special
   Award

Married to Jean Desprès, an executive vice president of Coty, now retired. Left school at 14 to become apprentice to a milliner aunt; at 15 was apprentice in workrooms of Reboux, later at Maison Talbot, where she picked up pins and packed hats. Came to United States in 1924; worked one week behind millinery counter at Macy's; with a partner opened millinery shop in the West Eighties. Her partner left; Daché moved to Broadway and 86th Street in the same neighborhood as HATTIE CARNEGIE; next went to 485 Madison Avenue and finally to her own nine-story building on East 57th Street which contained showroom, workrooms and living quarters, a duplex apartment on the roof. Closed business in 1968 upon her husband's retirement.

Her major contributions were draped turbans, brimmed hats molded to the head, half hats, visored caps for war workers, colored snoods, romantic-massed flower shapes. By 1949 she was designing dresses to go with her hats, also lingerie, loungewear, gloves, hosiery, even a wired strapless bra. She later designed men's shirts and ties.

Her influence has been felt by such designers as HALSTON; Kenneth worked in her beauty salon before going into business for himself.

1940

Daves, Jessica

(Fashion editor)

BORN: Cartersville, Georgia,
20 February 1898.
DIED: New York City, 1974.

MEMBER:
The Fashion Group
(president, 1964–1965);
National Press Club
AWARDS:
French Legion of Honor
Italian Order of Merit
PUBLICATIONS:
The Vogue Book of Menus. New
York: Harper & Row,
1964.
*Ready-Made Miracle: The Story
of American Fashion for the
Millions.* New York: G.P.
Putnam's Sons, 1967.
The World in Vogue. Compiled
by The Viking Press and
Vogue, 1963. Jessica Daves
and Alexander Liberman,
editors for *Vogue;* Bryan
Holme and Katherine
Tweed for Viking Press.

Married Robert A. Parker, a writer, who died in 1970; no children.

Arrived New York in 1921; worked for three years in advertising department of Best & Co., then at different New York stores including Saks Fifth Avenue, writing fashion copy, learning fashion merchandising firsthand.

Went to *Vogue* magazine in 1933 as fashion merchandising editor. Ability spotted by EDNA WOOLMAN CHASE, then editor-in-chief. Became managing editor in 1936; editor of American *Vogue* in 1946, editor-in-chief in 1952, upon Mrs. Chase's retirement. A director of Condé Nast Publications from 1946 until her retirement in 1963. Served one year as editorial consultant and then worked on specialized books until November 1966.

In person Miss Daves was short and plump, she dressed well but her figure precluded real chic. Her manner was warm, reflecting her genuine interest in and concern for people; her voice retained charming overtones of her southern origin. In her later years she became rather regal with something of a queen mother effect.

Under her direction *Vogue* assumed a more serious tone and ran more articles of intellectual interest than before. This reflected Miss Daves's conviction that women, while very much interested in clothes, do have other, more substantial concerns. The years of her editorship coincided with a phenomenal growth of the American ready-to-wear industry. She recognized its increasing importance and acknowledged the limited market for top-priced French designer models, broadening coverage of domestic ready-to-wear and including more moderately priced clothes. She is remembered for clear headedness and sound judgment—of all the great fashion editors she was probably the most astute businesswoman. She was an accomplished writer and editor, could fix a piece of ailing copy in minutes.

de Rauch, Madeleine

(French couturière)

An accomplished sportswoman who in the 1920s began designing for herself in order to have the proper clothes for active sports. When friends persuaded her to make clothes for them, opened business called House of Friendship, employing a single worker. With help of two sisters, business grew until she established the House of de Rauch overlooking the Cours de Reine. It closed in 1973.

De Rauch was known for beautiful, wearable, functional clothes. Soft fabrics were handled with great fluidity, draped close at the top of the figure, wide necklines were often framed with folds or tucks. Plaids, checks and stripes were treated with simplicity and precision, so perfectly done they seemed to have been assembled on a drawing board.

Dessès, Jean

(French couturier)

BORN: Alexandria,
  Egypt,
  6 August 1904.
DIED: Athens,
  Greece,
  2 August 1970.

1949

Of Greek ancestry. From childhood he was interested in beautiful clothes; at age 9 designed a dress for his mother.

Attended school in Alexandria; studied law in Paris; switched to fashion design in 1925. For twelve years worked for Jane on the rue de la Paix; opened own establishment in 1937 on avenue George V, and in 1948 on avenue Matignon, in a mansion formerly owned by Alexandre Eiffel, designer of the famous tower.

Dessès made his first trip to the United States in 1949, entering into manufacturing agreements with two American firms. He admired American women and in 1950 designed a lower-priced line for them called "Jean Dessès Diffusion," seen as the beginning of mass production in French couture.

He was a gentle, refined man who loved luxury, collected Oriental art objects, was inspired in his work by native costumes seen in museums on his travels, especially in Greece and Egypt. Dessès designed directly on the dummy, draping fabrics himself. He is remembered primarily for draped evening gowns of chiffon and mousseline in beautiful colors, and for the subtlety with which he handled fur. Customers included Princess Margaret, the Duchess of Kent, and the Queen of Greece.

Gave up couture business in 1965, because of ill health and returned to Greece, where in semi-retirement he ran a boutique until his death.

Dior, Christian _____

(French couturier)

BORN: Granville, Normandy, France, 31 January 1905.
DIED: Montecatini, Italy, 24 October 1957.

AWARDS:
  1947—Neiman-Marcus Award
  1956—Parsons Medal for Distinguished Achievement
PUBLICATIONS:
  Christian Dior and I. New York: E. P. Dutton & Company, Inc., 1957

Son of well-to-do manufacturer of fertilizer and chemicals. Attended School of Political Science; had many friends among young painters, writers, and musicians.

After obligatory military service in 1927, opened small art gallery with friend in 1928. Family ruined by depression in 1931; Dior traveled to Russia the same year, returning to find partner also ruined. Led hand-to-mouth existence for the next few years and in 1934 became seriously ill and had to leave Paris for enforced rest in France and Spain.

Discovered a desire to create something himself; learned tapestry weaving and design. Returned in 1935 and at age 30, unable to find any kind of job, started making design sketches; also did fashion illustrations for *Le Figaro.* Sold first sketches that year for twenty francs each.

Early hat designs were successful, dresses less so. In 1937, after two-year struggle to improve his dresses, sold several sketches to ROBERT PIGUET who then asked Dior to make a number of dresses for an upcoming collection and in 1938 hired him as a designer. Dior was mobilized in 1939, stationed in south of France when Paris fell in June 1940. Asked by Piguet to come back to work, but Dior delayed return to Paris until end of 1941, by which time another designer had been hired. Went to work for LUCIEN LELONG, a much larger house; was there when liberation came.

Introduced in 1945 to Marcel Boussac, French financier and race horse owner, who was looking for someone to take over direction of an ailing couture house he owned. Dior decided against project, persuaded Boussac to back him instead. Left Lelong at end of 1946, presented wildly successful first collection in spring 1947.

The "New Look" was, in essence, a polished continuation of the rounded line seen in the first postwar collections and appeared at the same time at a number of design houses. Dior's was a dream of flower-like women wearing clothes with rounded shoulders, feminine busts, tiny waists, enormous spreading skirts, everything exquisitely made of the best materials available. He continued to produce collection after collection of beautiful clothes, each evolving from the one before: in 1952 the Sensuous line which began to loosen the waist; in 1954 the H-line, which freed the waistline more, a movement continued with the A- and Y-lines in 1955.

Meanwhile, Christian Dior, Inc. had become a vast international merchandising operation with the Dior label on jewelry, scarves, men's ties, furs, stockings, gloves. A simpler, less expensive boutique line was introduced in 1948, the same year he established Christian Dior-New York (closed in 1975); Dior-Delman shoes were designed by Roger Vivier.

Dior described himself as a silent, slow Norman, shy and reticent by nature, strongly attached to his friends, a lover of good food. For relaxation and pleasure he read history and archaeology, played cards; his chief passion was for architecture. Like many designers he was superstitious, believed in the importance of luck and consulted fortune tellers on the major decisions of his life.

Since his death in 1957, the House of Dior has continued under the direction of other designers: YVES SAINT LAURENT until 1960, and from 1960 with MARC BOHAN, also responsible for the French-made Christian Dior Boutique ready-to-wear.

The "New Look," 1947

Erté (born Romain de Tirtoff) ——————————

(Fashion artist and designer)

BORN: St. Petersburg, Russia,
10 November 1892.

PUBLICATIONS:
ERTÉ Things I Remember (an
autobiography). London:
Peter Owen Limited,
1975.

Son of admiral in Russian Imperial Navy. Studied painting in Russia; went to Paris, 1912, to study at Académie Julian; got a job sketching for PAUL POIRET. Took name from French pronunciation of his initials R.T., or "air-tay." Went on to design for the theater and opera, in 1913; doing costumes for such actresses as Mary Garden and Ganna Walska. Illustrated for *La Gazette du Bon Ton,* Paris, 1914; produced covers and illustrations for *Harper's Bazaar* from 1915 to the 1930s. Designed for Folies Bergère, 1919–1930.

Came to United States in the 1920s to work for Ziegfeld and other impresarios; tried Hollywood briefly in 1925 but was impatient with financial restrictions and returned to Paris after eight months. During this time he created beautiful and esoteric costumes for several films, including *The Mystic, Ben Hur,* and King Vidor's *La Bohème.*

In 1967, to celebrate his 80th birthday, Erté selected over a hundred of his designs for clothes, jewelry and accessories, to be shown in London and at the Grosvenor Gallery in New York. The exhibition contained some of the most elegant and individual designs of the Art Deco period and was a fascinating opportunity to see how an artist, rather than a dressmaker, approached the problem of dressing. The New York exhibition was bought in its entirety by the Metropolitan Museum of Art.

Erté lives in Paris, still enthusiastic and interested in every aspect of decorative art.

Fairchild, John ——————————

(American publisher)

BORN: Newark, New Jersey,
6 March 1927.

AWARDS:
1975—French Order of
Merit

Attended Kent Preparatory School in Connecticut; entered Princeton University, 1946. Married Jill Lipsky, 1950; four children. After college went to work for Fairchild Publications, third generation in then family-owned business. Covered general retail news in New York City area; named successively head of London and Paris bureaus. Returned from Europe in 1960, since then has been publisher of *Women's Wear*

PUBLICATIONS:
The Fashionable Savages.
Garden City, New York:
Doubleday & Co., Inc.,
1965.

Daily. In early 1970s began publishing *W,* a bi-weekly aimed at consumers; chairman of board of Fairchild Publications since 1970.

Fairchild first attracted attention during his Paris sojourn. He developed a lively, informal writing style, panning collections he did not like, praising his favorites extravagantly. In order to get scoops, he cultivated news sources among employees of the great couture houses where secrecy has always been a sacred law; he printed fashion news as soon as he got hold of it, ignored official release dates set by the couture.

Under his direction, *Women's Wear Daily* evolved from a colorless, stodgy trade paper to a gossipy, readable publication followed by both trade and consumers as much for its reportage of people and happenings as for its news of fashion. The fashion side of the paper was not neglected, however, as Fairchild developed first-rate artists and devoted generous amounts of space to their work, supplementing sketches with photographs. He personally coined catchy words and phrases to describe styles and personalities and encouraged his writers to do the same. "The beautiful people" is a Fairchild phrase that came into general use.

Lives in Manhattan; travels frequently.

Fath, Jacques

(French couturier)

BORN: Lafitte (near Paris),
France, 12 September 1912.
DIED: Paris, France,
14 November 1954.

AWARDS:
1949—Neiman-Marcus
Award

Son of an Alsatian businessman, grandson of a painter. Showed early talent in costume design for the theater and films. Opened couture house in 1937, with small collection of twenty models.

Kept house open during World War II and was immensely successful for the next seventeen years; expanded his salon after liberation from a single workroom with one fitter to an establishment with six hundred employees. Name Fath went into perfume, scarves, stockings, millinery. Formed company in the United States, 1951; entered into agreements with other United States companies for use of his name.

Robe crêpe imprimé

T. Fath

1947

Fath did not sew or cut but draped material while assistants sketched. His clothes were flattering, feminine, sexy, with hourglass shapes, plunging necklines, swathed hips or full pleated skirts, wide cape collars.

Handsome and personable, with a flair for publicity and showmanship, he became one of the most popular designers of the 1940s and early 1950s. He loved parties and with his wife, actress Geneviève de Bruyère, gave elaborate entertainments at their Corbeville chateau. He died of leukemia at the age of 42. His wife continued the business for a few years, closing it in 1957.

Ferragamo, Salvatore

(Italian shoemaker)

BORN: Bonito (near Naples), Italy, June 1898
DIED: Fiumetto, Italy, 7 August 1960

AWARDS:
1947—Neiman-Marcus Award
PUBLICATIONS:
Shoemaker of Dreams (autobiography). England: George G. Harrap & Co. Ltd., 1957.

Son of small property owner. Opened own shoemaking shop in Bonito at age 13; emigrated to United States in 1923; studied mass shoemaking techniques; opened shop in Hollywood, designing and making shoes by hand for such film stars as Dolores Del Rio, Pola Negri, Gloria Swanson. Also maintained a successful business in factory-made shoes.

Returned to Italy. Opened business in Florence in 1936 and by 1960 had ten factories in Italy and Great Britain. Since his death in 1960, the business has been carried on by daughters, Fiamma and Giovanna, and son, Ferruccio. In addition to shoes, the Ferragamo name appears on handbags, scarves, ready-to-wear; there are free-standing boutiques in Europe and the

United States as well as boutiques in major United States specialty stores.

Ferragamo is said to have originated the wedge heel, the platform sole, and the Lucite heel. Early designs are fantasies of shape, color, and fabric; in recent years the emphasis has been on ladylike, conservative styling, and comfortable fit.

Fogarty, Anne

(American designer)

BORN: Pittsburgh, Pennsylvania, 2 February 1919.

AWARDS:
1951—Coty American Fashion Critics' Special Award (dresses)
1952—Neiman-Marcus Award
MEMBER:
Council of Fashion Designers of America
The Fashion Group
PUBLICATIONS:
Wife-Dressing. New York: Julian Messner, Inc., 1959.

Attended Carnegie Tech; moved to New York. Married Tom Fogarty in 1940; divorced; two children. Married Richard Kollmar who died in 1971.

Worked as model and stylist. Between 1948 and 1957 designed junior-size dresses for Youth Guild, Margot, Inc.; later for Saks Fifth Avenue. Started Anne Fogarty Inc. in 1962, closed in the middle 1970s.

Became prominent in early 1950s; best known for "paper-doll" silhouette; for crinoline petticoats under full-skirted shirtdresses with tiny waists; in 1958 for the "camise," a chemise gathered from a high yoke; for lounging coveralls. In early 1970s showed peasant look with ruffled shirts, long skirts with ruffled hems, hot pants under long quilted skirts. Also designed lingerie, jewelry, shoes, hats, coats, suits.

Fontana

(Italian couture house)

Founded 1907 in Parma, moved to Rome, full name is Sorelle Fontana, or in English, Fontana Sisters. Headed by mother, Amabile, assisted by daughters Micol and Zoe as designers, Giovanna in charge of boutique. One of leading Italian houses in 1950s, noted for evening gowns, delicate handwork, asymmetric lines and interesting necklines. In 1957 gave scholarship awards and three-month apprenticeships to American students. Did costumes for Ava Gardner in *The Barefoot Contessa.*

Still in business in late 1970s.

Fortuny, Mariano
(born Mariano Fortuny y Madrazo)

(Italian fabric and fashion designer)

BORN: Granada, Spain, 1871.
DIED: 1949.

Son of painter. Studied painting, drawing, sculpture, then chemistry and dyes. Moved to Venice at turn of century. Invented process for printing color and metals on fabrics to achieve an effect of brocade, velvet, and tapestry. Fortuny fabrics still used in interior design, manufactured in Venice.

In fashion, Fortuny became famous for his silk tea gowns in rich and subtle colors, simple columns of mushroom pleating in one or two pieces, slipped over the head and tied at the waist by thin silk cords. A status symbol of the 1930s, the gowns are now rare collector's pieces cherished by those who are of necessity, both rich and slender.

Hartnell, Norman

(English designer)

BORN: London, England, 12 June 1901.
DIED: Windsor, England, 8 June 1979.

AWARDS:
  1947—Neiman-Marcus Award
PUBLICATIONS:
  Silver and Gold (autobiography). London: Evans Brothers, 1955.
  Royal Courts of Fashion. London: Cassell & Co. Ltd., 1971.

Educated Cambridge University where he showed talent for sketching, designed costumes for undergraduate play. Began dress designing with his sister in 1923. In 1927 showed clothes for first time in Paris; success came with second Paris showing in 1930 which brought many orders from American and Canadian buyers, among others.

Couture house became largest in London, dressmaker by appointment to HM the Queen and to HM Queen Elizabeth, the Queen Mother. Produced coronation gowns for Queen Elizabeth II in 1953. Known for well-tailored suits and coats in British and French woolens and tweeds, and for lavishly embroidered evening gowns. By 1970s was making clothes in leather, designing furs and men's fashions.

Was knighted in 1977.

James, Charles

(American designer)

BORN: London, England, c. 1905.
DIED: New York City, 23 September 1978.

Father was a colonel in British army; mother's family prominent in Chicago. Educated in England and America. Began fashion career in 1928 in Chicago making hats; after two years moved to New York, then to London, where he produced a small dress collec-

1960

1961

Travel coat

Charles James 61

AWARDS:
Coty American Fashion
Critics Award:
1950—"Winnie"
1954—Special Award
1953—Neiman-Marcus
Award

tion which he brought back to New York. Returned to London where he remained to live and work until moving to Paris around 1934 to open his own couture business.

In Paris he formed close friendships with many legendary couture figures including PAUL POIRET and also CHRISTIAN DIOR, whose obituary he wrote for *The New York Post.* He admired SCHIAPARELLI in her

29

unadorned period; ALIX GRÈS was his favorite designer because she thinks, as he did, in terms of shape and sculptural movement. He returned to New York around 1939; operated his own custom design house in the 1940s and 1950s. Retired from couture in 1958 to devote himself to painting and sculpture; conducted costume design seminars in 1960 at Rhode Island School of Design and at Pratt Institute; designed a mass-produced line for E. J. Korvette in 1962. Along the way he invented new techniques for dress patterns, created a dress form, jewelry designs and even furniture. In the 1970s occupied himself with preparing his archives.

James was always a daring innovator, a sculptor with cloth, each design beginning with a certain "shape," hours spent on the exact placement of a seam. Bold and imaginative, his designs depend on intricate cut and precise seaming rather than on trim. He was noted for his handling of heavy silks and fine cloths, for his batwing, oval cape coat, for bouffant ball gowns, for dolman wraps and asymmetrical shapes. In 1937 his short white satin evening coat filled with eiderdown appeared on the cover of *Harper's Bazaar;* Dali called it "the first soft sculpture." His designs are in the costume collections of the Brooklyn Museum, the Smithsonian Institution, the Fashion Institute of Technology. In the opinion of many students of fashion, he was a genius, stormy and unpredictable, fiercely independent. His ideas and influence are still felt today.

Klein, Anne (born Hannah Golofski) ——————

(American designer)

BORN: Brooklyn, New York, 1923.
DIED: New York City, 19 March 1974.

AWARDS:
Coty American Fashion Critics' Award:
1955—"Winnie"
1969—Return Award

Married and divorced Ben Klein; married Chip Rubenstein. Got first job on Seventh Avenue at age 15 as freelance sketcher; joined Varden Petites a year later. In 1948 she and Ben Klein formed Junior Sophisticates; she designed for Mallory Leathers in 1965; opened Anne Klein Studio on West 57th Street. In 1968, with Chip Rubenstein and Sanford Smith, formed Anne Klein & Co., now wholly owned by Takihyo Corporation of Japan.

Klein became known early in her career for her pioneering work in transforming junior-size clothes

1971

1971—Hall of Fame
1959, 1969—Neiman-Marcus
Award

from little-girl cuteness to adult sophistication. At Junior Sophisticates: the skimmer dress with jacket; full-skirted dresses with wasp waists; long, pleated plaid skirts with blazers; grey flannel used with white satin. At Anne Klein & Co. her emphasis was on investment sportswear at healthy prices: an interrelated wardrobe of blazers, skirts, pants, sweaters; long, slinky, hooded jersey dresses for evening. Licenses include shoes, belts, scarves, watches, bed linens.

Since her death, the firm has continued with DONNA KARAN and LOUIS DELL'OLIO as co-designers.

Lanvin, Jeanne

(French couturière)

BORN: Brittany, France, 1867.
DIED: Paris, France,
6 July 1946.

AWARDS:
French Legion of Honor

Eldest of a journalist's ten children; apprenticed at 13; started as milliner at 23. First successes were with dresses she designed for young daughter, Marie-Blanche. These designs were admired by customers and bought by them for their own children. As the children grew up, Lanvin continued to design for them, evolving into the House of Lanvin, Faubourg St. Honoré.

Lanvin's designs were noted for a youthful quality, often reflecting the influence of costumes of her native Brittany. She collected costume books, daguerreotypes, historical plates, and drew inspiration from them, notably for the *robes de style* for which she was known, and for her wedding gowns. She preferred plain fabrics and decorated them herself, maintaining a department for machine embroidery under the charge of her brother. The house produced women's sport clothes, furs, children's wear, lingerie, and in 1926 a men's wear department was established under the direction of her nephew, Maurice Lanvin. There were branch shops in French resorts. Lanvin was one of the first couturiers to establish a perfume business; perfumes were "My Sin," "Arpège," "Rumeur," "Prétexte," and after her death, "Crescendo."

Mme. Lanvin represented France and the couture at international expositions such as the 1939 New York World's Fair; was elected President of the Haute Couture at the Paris International Exhibition in 1937.

She was famous for her use of quilting and stitching, for her embroideries and for the discreet use of sequins. For fantasy evening gowns with metallic embroideries, tea gowns, dinner pajamas, dolman wraps, capes, Zouave bloomer skirts in 1936.

After her death in 1946 the House of Lanvin continued under the direction of her family, including her daughter, the Comtesse de Polignac. It is now owned by Bernard Lanvin and his wife. Designers have been Antonio del Castillo, 1950–1962, and from 1963, JULES-FRANÇOIS CRAHAY.

Lelong, Lucien

(French couturier)

BORN: Paris, France,
11 October 1889.
DIED: Anglet (near Biarritz),
France, 10 May 1958.

Father was a couturier. Lelong trained for a business career but decided on couture in 1914; called into army two days before presentation of first collection. Was wounded in World War I and in hospital for a year; received Croix de Guerre.

Entered father's business in 1918, took control soon after; established Parfums Lucien Lelong, 1926; started "Editions" department of ready-to-wear, 1934. Elected president of Chambre Syndicale de la Couture in 1937; held post for ten years, including the occupation period when the Germans wanted to move the entire French dressmaking industry to Berlin and Vienna. Lelong managed to frustrate the plan and guided the couture safely through the war years. A serious illness in 1947 caused him to close his couture house; he continued to direct his perfume business.

Lelong was considered a director of designers rather than a designer himself. PIERRE BALMAIN, CHRISTIAN DIOR, GIVENCHY, JEAN SCHLUMBERGER, all worked for him; Dior praised him as a good friend and a generous employer. From 1919 to 1948, his house produced distinguished collections of beautiful clothes for a conservative clientele. Lelong believed strongly in honest workmanship and good needlework and it was his credo that a Lelong creation would hold together until its fabrics wore out.

He was an accomplished painter, sculptor, composer and sportsman.

Mainbocher
(born Main Rousseau Bocher)

(American couturier)

BORN: Chicago, Illinois,
24 October 1890.
DIED: Munich, Germany,
26 December 1976.

Of French-Dutch and Scottish-English descent. Encouraged by mother to study art, also yearned for an operatic career. Attended Lewis Institute, University of Chicago, Chicago Academy of Fine Arts. Went to *Vogue*'s 1914 "Fashion Fête," taken by manufacturer for whom he was sketching at the time. In 1917 went to Paris with American ambulance unit; remained after the war to study singing. Went to work in Paris as fashion illustrator for *Harper's Bazaar* in 1922, then to French *Vogue*, where he remained from 1923 to 1929, as fashion editor and briefly, as full editor.

Mainbocher, 1931
(Courtesy of *Harper's
Bazaar* © 1931,
The Hearst Corp.)

In 1929 opened Paris salon under name Mainbocher and in his first year, it is said, he introduced the strapless evening gown and persuaded French textile manufacturers to again set up double looms and weave wide widths not produced since before the war. He made a success with elegant, wearable clothes; the Duchess of Windsor, whose wedding dress he made, and Lady Mendl were among his clients. Left Paris on outbreak of World War II; opened New York couture house in 1939, becoming the designer with most snob appeal for the rich and conservative until he closed his business in 1971.

Mainbocher was noted for a nearly infallible sense of fashion and as a creator of high-priced clothes of quiet good taste, simplicity and understatement. Elegant evening clothes were his forte: long, high-waisted ball gowns of lace or transparent fabrics; the short evening dress; beaded evening sweaters with jeweled buttons; tweed dinner suits with delicate blouses. He did a great deal with pastel gingham; his signature accessories were pearl chokers, short white kid gloves, plain pumps. Designed uniforms for American Red Cross, the WAVES, SPARS, Girl Scouts.

Known as a skillful editor of the designs of others as well as a creator, Mainbocher has been ranked with MOLYNEUX, SCHIAPARELLI, LELONG. His design philosophy has been widely quoted: "The responsibility and challenge . . . is to consider the design and the woman at the same time. Women should look beautiful, rather than just trendful."

McCardell, Claire

(American designer)

BORN: Frederick, Maryland,
24 May 1905.
DIED: New York City,
23 March 1958.

AWARDS:
Coty American Fashion
Critics' Award:
1944—"Winnie"
1958—Hall of Fame
(posthumous)

Daughter of state senator. Interest in clothes appeared early—with paper dolls as a child, with her own clothes as a teenager. Attended Hood College for women in Maryland. Studied fashion illustration for two years at Parsons School of Design in New York and for one year in Paris. Returned to New York; painted lampshades for B. Altman & Co.; modeled briefly.

Joined Robert Turk Inc. as model and assistant designer in 1929; in 1931 went with Turk to Townley Frocks Inc. Continued as designer after his death,

Claire McCardell, 1944

String-Tied
Empire Line

The Popover

The Draped
Bathing Suit

Railroad-Stitched Denim /
Bib-Front, Low-Back

1948—Neiman-Marcus
Award
1950—National Women's
Press Club
1956—Parsons Medal for
Distinguished Achievement
PUBLICATIONS:
What Shall I Wear?. New
York: Simon & Schuster,
Inc., 1956.

until 1938; resigned and went to Hattie Carnegie, 1938–1940; returned to Townley Frocks, first as designer, then as designer-partner from 1940 until her death.

McCardell designed specifically for the American woman with her full schedule of work and play. Her philosophy was simple—clothes should be clean in line, functional, comfortable, and appropriate to the occasion. They should fit well, flow naturally with the body, and of course, be attractive to look at. Buttons had to button, sashes were required to be long enough to not only tie but wrap around and around.

She is credited with originating the American Look, forerunner of today's easy, travel-oriented clothes.

She picked up details from men's clothing and work clothes, such as large pockets, blue-jeans stitching, trouser pleats, rivets, side trouser pockets, gripper fastenings; worked with sturdy cotton denim, ticking, gingham, and wool jersey. Several themes recurred, many of them for fun: the diaper bathing suit, colored zippers meant to show, spaghetti ties, and surprise juxtapositions of color.

Among her innovations were the monastic dress with natural shoulders and tied waist, 1938; harem pajamas, 1937; the Popover; a straight, slip-on shift; the kitchen dinner dress; ballet slippers with day clothes.

Designed sunglasses, infants' and children's wear, children's shoes, and costume jewelry.

Stanley Marcus described her as ". . . the master of the line, never the slave of the sequin. She is one of the few creative designers this country has ever produced."

Molyneux, Captain Edward

(English couturier)

BORN: Hampstead, England, 1894.
DIED: Monte Carlo, 22 March 1974.

Of upper class Irish-English birth, French ancestry. Art student, sportsman, officer in Duke of Wellington regiment. In 1911 won competition sponsored by Lucile (Lady Duff Gordon) and at age 17 was engaged to sketch for her dressmaking establishment. Went with her to the United States when she opened branches in New York and Chicago, remained until the outbreak of World War I. Joined British army in 1914; wounded three times, resulting eventually in loss of sight of one eye; won Military Cross for bravery; earned rank of captain in 1917.

In 1919 opened own couture house in Paris at 14, rue Royale; later moved to No. 5 next to Maxim's. Branches followed: Monte Carlo, 1925; Cannes, 1927; London, 1932, with his sister in charge. Acquired a distinguished clientele including Princess Marina, the Duchess of Windsor, such stage and film personalities as Lynn Fontanne, Gertrude Lawrence, and Merle Oberon. Showed excellent head for business; enjoyed nightclubs and gambling; assembled fine collection of Impressionist paintings.

Escaped France in 1940 by fishing boat from Bordeaux; worked out of London house during World War II, turning over profits to national defense. Established international canteens in London and Paris. One of original members of Incorporated Society of London Fashion Designers, 1942. Designs were sold to United States during war.

Reopened Paris house in 1946, adding furs, lingerie, millinery, and perfumes. Because of ill health closed London house, 1949; turned over Paris operation to Jacques Griffe, 1950. Retired to Montego Bay, Jamaica, West Indies, devoting himself to painting and travel.

Persuaded by financial interests behind perfumes to reopen in Paris as Studio Molyneux for reproductions only; brought first ready-to-wear collection to United States, February 1965. In 1967 turned over design reins to his nephew, John Tullis. Retired again, this time to Biot, near Antibes.

Molyneux is remembered for well-bred, fluid, elegant clothes with a pure, uncluttered line. Printed silk suits with pleated skirts; timeless, softly tailored navy blue suits, coats, capes with accents of bright Gauguin pink and bois de rose; for the use of zippers in 1937 to mold the figure; for handkerchief point skirts and ostrich trims.

He financed dressmaking schools for French workers, gave generously of his personal resources—money, time, and energy.

Norell, Norman (born Norman Levinson) ————

(American designer)

BORN: Noblesville, Indiana, 1900.
DIED: New York City, 25 October 1972.

AWARDS:
Norell's career was distinguished by a number of "firsts":
Coty American Fashion Critics' Award:
1943—First "Winnie"
1951—First Return Award

During his childhood, family moved to Indianapolis where his father owned a haberdashery. From early boyhood Norman's ambition was to be an artist and in 1919 he came to New York to study painting at the Parsons School of Design; switched to costume design and graduated from Pratt Institute. First assignment was to design costumes for Rudolph Valentino film, *The Sainted Devil;* did Gloria Swanson's costumes for film, *Zaza,* then joined staff of Brooks Costume Company.

In 1924 went to work for dress manufacturer Charles Armour, remaining until 1928 when he joined HATTIE CARNEGIE. Stayed with Carnegie until 1940

Norman Norell and models, 1960

1958—First to be
     elected to Hall of Fame
11 June 1962—First
     designer to receive
     Honorary Degree of
     Doctor of Fine Arts,
     conferred upon him by
     Pratt Institute, Brooklyn,
     in recognition of his
     influence on American
     design and taste, and for
     his valuable counseling
     and guidance to students
     of design
1942—Neiman-Marcus
     Award
1956—Parsons Medal for
     Distinguished Achievement
1972—City of New York
     Bronze Medallion (presented
     at the retrospective by the
     City's Commissioner of
     Consumer Affairs, Bess
     Myerson)
MEMBER:
   Council of Fashion
     Designers of America
     (founder and president)

when Traina-Norell was established. This association lasted nineteen years, at which time Norell left to become president of his own firm, Norman Norell, Inc. The first collection was presented in June 1960.

From his very first collection under the Traina-Norell label the designer established himself as a major talent, quickly becoming known for a lithe, cleanly proportioned silhouette, an audacious use of rich fabrics, for faultless workmanship, precise tailoring, and purity of line. Over the years he maintained his leadership, setting numerous trends. His long, shimmering sequined dresses were treasured by women for ten years or more, so simple that they did not go out of date, worn as long as their owners could fit into them. He lined cloth coats with fur for day and evening or spangled them with sequins; topped long evening skirts with sweaters; revived the chemise; introduced the smoking robe; perfected jumpers and pantsuits. Introduced "Norell" perfume, made in America and a major success.

On the eve of his retrospective show at the Metropolitan Museum of Art, 15 October 1972, he suffered a stroke and died ten days later.

His company continued for a brief period with GUSTAVE TASSELL as designer; the perfume is still available.

Paquin, House of _____

(French couture house)

French couture house located on rue de la Paix, founded 1891 by M. and Mme. Isidore Paquin. Mme. Paquin, who trained at Maison Rouff, was one of couture's great artists, her husband was a banker and businessman. M. Paquin died young, the business was carried on by Mme. Paquin until she sold out to an English firm and retired. She died in 1936; the house closed in July 1956.

Paquin name was synonymous with elegance during the first decade of the twentieth century, its reputation for beautiful designs enhanced by the decor of the establishment, the lavishness of its showings and of the Paquins' social life. Management of the house and its relations with its employees were excellent, some workers remaining for more than forty years. Department heads were women. The Paquin standards were so high that there was always a demand from other couture houses for any employees deciding to leave.

Mme. Paquin was the first woman to achieve importance in haute couture and was president of the fashion section of the 1900 Paris Exposition. Hers was the first couture house to open foreign branches, the first in London in 1912, later in Madrid and Buenos Aires. She was first to take mannequins to the opera and the races, as many as ten in the same costume. She claimed not to make any two dresses exactly alike, individualizing each model for the woman for whom dress was made. Customers included queens of Belgium, Portugal and Spain as well as the *grandes cocottes* of the era.

Specialties were fur-trimmed tailored suits and coats; furs (house was credited with being first to make fur garments that were soft and supple); lingerie; evening dresses in white, gold lamé, pale green; blue serge suits with gold braid and buttons. Accessories were made in-house; first perfume appeared in 1939.

Partos, Emeric ''Imre'' —————————

(Designer specializing in furs)

BORN: Budapest, Hungary, 1905.
DIED: New York City, 1975.

AWARDS:
1957—Coty American Fashion Critics' Special Award (furs)

Moved to France as a young boy; served in French army during World War II and in the underground movement where he met Alex Maguy, a couturier who also designed for the theater. Joined Maguy, designed coats and also ballet costumes. Was a friend of CHRISTIAN DIOR, whom he considered the greatest living designer. Went to work for Dior in 1947, creating dresses, coats, suits. Was wooed away in 1950 by Maximilian, New York, and worked for them designing furs for five years before moving to Bergdorf Goodman to head their fur department. Continued with Bergdorf's until his death at age 70.

At Bergdorf's he was given a free hand with the most expensive pelts available. He showed a sense of fantasy and fun with intarsia furs such as a white mink jacket inlaid with flowers in colored mink, mink dyed in stripes or worked in beige-and-white box shapes in coats that could be shortened by removing sections. He also innovated with raincoats in silk or cotton poplin slipcovering mink coats; was noted for subtle, beautifully cut classics in fine minks, sables, broadtail.

Partos was one of the first to treat furs as ready-to-wear, always designed clothes to coordinate with his furs. He was a prolific source of ideas, noted for his theatrics but also as a master of construction and detail, a favorite with conservative customers as well as with personalities such as Barbra Streisand.

Patou, Jean

(French couturier)

BORN: 1887.
DIED: Paris, France,
March 1936.

Of French Basque origin. Before World War I had small house called "Parry." Success arrived in 1914 when an American retailer bought his entire collection. Mobilization for war caused cancellation of first major showing scheduled for August 1914, and Patou served four years in army as captain of Zouaves. Reopened under his own name in 1919 on rue Saint Florentin.

From the start Patou's clothes were a success with private clients. They had simplicity and elegance and looked as if they were intended to be worn by real women rather than by mannequins only. He was also an excellent showman and in 1925, to attract the lucrative business of American store buyers, brought six American models to Paris, using them alongside his French mannequins to show the collection. He instituted gala champagne evening openings; had a cocktail bar in his shop; chose exquisite bottles for his perfumes. In 1929, while change was certainly in the air, he is given credit for being first to lengthen skirts, dropping them dramatically to the ankle, and returning the waistline to its normal position. He was among the first couturiers to have colors and fabrics produced especially for him.

In person, Patou was tall, handsome, gracious, fond of the world of sport and fashion. He admired American business methods and introduced daily staff meetings, a profit-sharing plan for executives and a bonus system for mannequins. He was a director of designers as well as a creator.

After his death, the house remained open under the direction of his brother-in-law, Raymond Barbas, with

Jean Patou, 1929 (Courtesy of *Harper's Bazaar* © 1929, The Hearst Corp.)

a series of resident designers including: MARC BOHAN, 1953; Michel Goma, 1963 to 1973; Angelo Tarlazzi, 1973; Roy Gonzalez, 1977.

Pedlar, Sylvia (born Sylvia Schlang) ──────────

(American lingerie designer)

BORN: New York City, 1901.
DIED: New York City, 26 February 1972.

MEMBER:
The Fashion Group
AWARDS:
Coty American Fashion Critics' Award:
1951—Special Award (lingerie)
1964—Return Special Award (lingerie)
1960—Neiman-Marcus Award

Studied at Cooper Union and the Art Students League. Married William A. Pedlar, who died the year before she did.

Founded Iris Lingerie in 1929; closed the firm in 1970 after forty-one years because, "the fun has gone out of our work now."

Pedlar was a gifted designer working in a difficult field. She specialized in soft, pure shapes that a woman of any age could wear. To her, comfort was the most important consideration in a gown. Iris Lingerie was known for exquisite fabrics and laces, perfectionist workmanship, as well as for the originality and beauty of the designs. Among her more famous creations were sleep togas, the bed-and-breakfast look, the bedside nightdress for the girl who sleeps nude and wants a little something decorative for waking hours. Her talent was recognized internationally and European designers such as DIOR, GIVENCHY, and EMILIO PUCCI would visit Iris to buy the Pedlar models.

Piguet, Robert ──────────────────────────

(French couturier)

BORN: Yverdon, Switzerland, 1901.
DIED: Lausanne, Switzerland, 22 February 1953.

Son of banker. Went to Paris at age 17 and from 1918 to 1928 studied design with conservative Redfern and brilliant POIRET, then opened own house on the rue du Cirque.

In 1933 moved to salon on the Rond-Point where a number of important fashion figures worked for him at the outset of their careers, including DIOR, 1937 to 1939 and GIVENCHY at age 17. JAMES GALANOS spent three months there working without salary. Dior said, "Robert Piguet taught me the virtues of simplicity. . . . how to suppress."

Piguet was an aristocratic, solitary man, super-sensitive, changeable, with a love of intrigue. Elegant and charming, a connoisseur of painting, literature, music. He suffered from ill health throughout his life, each summer leading a retired life in order to recuperate from the strain of his profession. He closed his house in 1951.

His clothes appealed to a younger customer. Perfectly cut, tailored suits with vests; black-and-white dresses of refined simplicity; afternoon dresses; fur-trimmed coats especially styled for petite women. He had a flair for dramatic effects. In the United States his influence was greater on wholesale than on custom order.

Poiret, Paul

(French couturier)

BORN: Paris, France,
   20 April 1879
DIED: Paris, France,
   28 April 1944.

PUBLICATIONS:
En Habillant l'Epoque. Paris:
   Grasset, 1930.
King of Fashion. Philadelphia,
   Pennsylvania: J. B.
   Lippincott Company,
   1931.
Revenez-Y. Paris: Gallemard,
   1932.
Art et Finance. Paris: Lutetia,
   1934.

Active 1904–1924. Born, lived, died in Paris. Married; five children. Apprenticed as youth to umbrella maker, taught himself costume sketching at home; sold first sketches to Mme. Cheruit at Raudnitz Soeurs. Joined Jacques Doucet in 1896, designing costumes for actresses, among them Réjane and Sarah Bernhardt; worked briefly for House of WORTH. Opened own firm in 1904.

Poiret was fascinated by the theater and the arts; friends included Diaghilev, Léon Bakst, Raoul Dufy, ERTÉ, Iribe. He was shrewd and egotistical; spent fortunes on fêtes, pageants and costume balls and on decorating his homes. He established a crafts school called "Martine" where Dufy for a while turned to textile design; was first couturier to present a perfume; in 1912 was first to travel to other countries to present his collection, taking along twelve mannequins. Co-founder in 1914 of Protective Association of French Dressmakers along with WORTH, PAQUIN, Cheruit, CALLOT SOEURS. Unable to adjust his style to changes brought about by World War I, Poiret went out of business in 1924, eventually abandoned his family and died of Parkinson's disease in a charity hospital.

Widely considered to be one of the greatest originators of feminine fashion, Poiret was extravagantly talented, with a flair for the bizarre and dramatic. While his forte was costume, the modern silhouette was to a great extent his invention; he freed women from corsets and petticoats and introduced the Directoire line, the first modern, straight-line dress. Yet he also invented the harem and hobble skirts, so narrow at the bottom that walking was almost impossible. His minaret skirt, inspired by and named after a play he costumed, spread worldwide; he designed a Russian tunic coat, straight in line and belted, made from sumptuous materials and reflecting the influence of the Rus-

1923

1913

sian ballet; his taste for orientalism showed up in his designs and he adorned his models with little turbans and tall aigrettes; he scandalized society in 1911 by taking mannequins to Auteuil races dressed in *jupe culottes,* also called Turkish trousers. His extraordinary imagination and his achievements flowered in the brilliant epoch of Diaghilev and Bakst and influenced the taste of two decades.

Pope, Virginia

(Fashion editor)

BORN: Chicago, Illinois,
29 June 1885.
DIED: New York City,
16 January 1978.

MEMBER:
New York Newspaper
Women's Club
The Fashion Group

At age 5 taken to Europe following father's death. Toured Europe with her mother for fifteen years, becoming fluent in French, German, and Italian, and familiar with the best of European art and music. Returned to Chicago in 1905. Joined Red Cross during World War I. Never married.

Tried various careers after the war: social work in Chicago, theater in New York where she and her mother moved in the early 1920s, book translations, writing. First published piece was article in *The New York Times* which she obtained by speaking German to one of the visiting Oberammergau Players from Germany; followed by articles about an Italian neighborhood which her knowledge of Italian helped her get. Joined *The Times* in 1925 as a member of the Sunday staff; eight years later became fashion editor, a position she held, and developed for twenty-two years. Following retirement from *The Times* in 1955, Miss Pope joined the staff of *Parade* magazine as fashion editor; her name remained on the masthead until her death.

In addition, she held the Edwin Goodman chair established by Bergdorf Goodman at the Fashion Institute of Technology, giving a course on "Fashion in Contemporary Living." She could frequently be seen on Seventh Avenue with her students, escorting them to fashion shows and behind the scenes to see how a business worked. And since she believed that exposure to culture was essential to a designer's development, she regularly took students to performances of the Metropolitan Opera.

As a journalist she is credited with practically inventing fashion reportage, being one of the first to look for news in the wholesale market. She considered the people who made clothes newsworthy at a time when only style changes originating in Paris were considered worth reporting; encouraged the American fashion industry in its early years, setting taste standards for young designers. At *The Times,* she originated the "Fashions of The Times" fashion show in 1942 as a showcase for American designers, staging it each fall for the next nine years. In 1952 this was transformed into a twice-yearly fashion supplement of the same name, still published by *The Times.*

While her personal style of dressing was of the establishment, she understood innovation and could look at clothes objectively. Referring to her appearance and her well-deserved "grande dame" reputation, a fellow editor once said, "she could play the Queen of England without a rehearsal."

Quant, Mary

(English designer)

BORN: Blackheath, Kent, England, 11 February 1934.

AWARDS:
O.B.E. (Order of the British Empire)
EXHIBITION:
"Mary Quant's London." London Museum, 1973–1974.
PUBLICATIONS:
Quant by Quant. London: Cassell & Co. Ltd., 1966.

Studied at Goldsmith's College of Art. Married in 1957 to Alexander Plunket Greene; one son.

After leaving school, opened small retail boutique called "Bazaar" in London's Chelsea district selling spirited, unconventional clothes such as tight pants, shaggy sweaters, thick stockings, and knickerbockers. Fame grew along with that of "swinging London"; she became full-scale designer and manufacturer with husband as business partner. Within ten years added cheaper "Ginger" line; designed for J. C. Penney chain in United States and for Puritan's Youthquake promotion. In the 1970s, while giving up the manufacturing role, she has continued to design, adding furs, lingerie, household linens and eyeglasses to her credits. Her cosmetic business continues in Europe and in the United States.

Quant was a leading figure in the youth revolution of the 1950s and 1960s. She is credited with starting the Chelsea or Mod Look of the mid 1950s and the miniskirts of the late 1960s; she used denim, colored flannel and vinyl in "kooky" clothes with a 1920s' flavor; colored tights; low-slung hipster pants. She pioneered with body stockings, hot pants and layered dressing.

Ricci, Nina (born Maria Nielli)

(French couturière)

BORN: Turin, Italy, 1883.
DIED: Paris, France, 29 November 1970.

Interested in clothes from childhood when she began dressing dolls. Went to Paris at age 13 to work as seamstress; by 1905 was designing models on live mannequins. Married to Louis Ricci, a jeweler; one son, Robert.

In 1932 opened own house, specializing in graceful

dresses of superb and detailed workmanship for mature, elegant women, and also producing trousseaus for young women. Was one of first to show lower-priced models in a boutique. Bottled her perfume, "L'Air du Temps," in a Lalique flacon with a frosted glass bird on the stopper.

Since 1945 the house has been managed by her son with various designers. Among them: JULES FRANÇOIS CRAHAY, 1954–1963; GÉRARD PIPART from 1963.

Rochas, Marcel

(French couturier)

BORN: Paris, France,
c. 1902.
DIED: Paris, France,
14 March 1955.

PUBLICATIONS:
Twenty-Five Years of Parisian Elegance, 1925–1950.
Paris, 1951.

Opened couture house about 1930 and according to legend, popularity was confirmed when eight women wore identical dresses from his house to the same party.

Rochas was known for young, daring designs, an abundance of fantastic ideas. He used as many as ten colors in combination; was lavish with lace, ribbon, tulle; showed a broad-shouldered, hourglass silhouette several years before the New Look; invented a waist-cincher to pull in the natural waist; packaged perfume "Femme" in black lace. He maintained a boutique for separates and accessories; designed for films.

He loved women and was married three times.

Schiaparelli, Elsa

(French couturière)

BORN: Rome, Italy,
10 September 1890.
DIED: Paris, France,
13 November 1973.

AWARDS:
1940—Neiman-Marcus
Award
PUBLICATIONS:
Shocking Life. New York:
E.P. Dutton & Co., Inc.,
1954.

Daughter of professor of Oriental languages. As child, traveled to Tunisia, later studied philosophy, wrote poetry and articles on music. Lived in Europe and in the United States until end of World War I. Married; daughter Marisa born in the United States; Marisa and Berry (Berynthia) Berenson are granddaughters.

In 1920, her husband having left her, she went to Paris and began designing sweaters which were made up for her by knitters in the Paris Armenian colony. By 1929 had business called "Pour le Sport" on the rue de la Paix; by 1930 was doing an estimated business of 120 million francs a year from twenty-six work-

The
Talleyrand
Suit

Evening Dress, Late 1930s

rooms employing two thousand people; opened boutique on the Place Vendome, 1935. She began with sport clothes, later included dresses and evening clothes.

Like CHANEL, Schiaparelli was more than a dressmaker, actually part of the brilliant artistic life of Paris in the 1920s and 1930s; had close friendships with artists such as Dali, Cocteau, Van Dongen, SCHLUMBERGER, and Man Ray. Highly creative and unconventional, she shocked the couture establishment in more ways than just her famous pink, using rough "working class" materials and innovative accessories, generating publicity.

She was spectacularly successful with avant-garde sweaters, worked with tattoo or skeleton motifs or with geometric patterns in bold colors; a signature hot-pink color she called "shocking"; her "Shocking" perfume in its hourglass, dressmaker dummy bottle; witty lapel ornaments in the shape of hands, teaspoons, hearts, angels; amusing novelties such as handbags that lit up or played tunes when opened and glowing phosphorescent brooches. She commissioned a fabric pattern designed from press clippings of articles about her then used the material in scarves, blouses, beachwear; pioneered in the use of synthetic fabrics. She changed the shape of the figure with broad, padded shoulders inspired by the London Guardsman's uniform; fastened clothing with colored zippers, jeweler-designed buttons, padlocks, clips, dog leashes. She showed little "doll hats" shaped like a lamb chop or a pink-heeled shoe, gloves that extended to the shoulders and turned into puffed sleeves. Even her simplest designs had elegance.

Following the fall of France, Schiaparelli came to the United States; returned to Paris after liberation, reopened house in 1945. First showed natural shoulder line, peplums, black dresses. Closed business in 1954; continued as consultant to companies licensed to produce hosiery, perfume, scarves under her name. Lived out retirement in Tunisia and in Paris, where she died.

Schiaparelli produced clothes of great elegance and extreme chic, but perhaps her major contribution was her vitality and sense of mischief, a reminder not to take it all too seriously.

Snow, Carmel (born Carmel White) _____

(Fashion editor)

BORN: Ireland, 1888.
DIED: New York City,
 9 May 1961.

AWARDS:
 1941—Neiman-Marcus
 Award
 1949—French Legion of
 Honor
 1954—Italian Star of
 Solidarity

PUBLICATIONS:
 Carmel Snow with Mary
 Louise Aswell. *The World of
 Carmel Snow.* New York:
 McGraw-Hill Book Co.,
 1962.

1958

Carmel's father died suddenly before a scheduled trip to the United States where he was to promote Irish industries at the 1893 Chicago World's Fair. His wife replaced him, then decided to remain in America and bring over her six children. She bought a dressmaking business in New York, Fox & Co., and made it a success; Carmel later became an assistant in the firm. Mrs. White was one of the exhibitors at *Vogue's* first "Fashion Fête" in 1914, making the dress worn on that occasion by *Vogue's* editor, EDNA WOOLMAN CHASE. A friendship developed and in 1921 Mrs. Chase offered Carmel a job in *Vogue's* fashion department. Married George Palen Snow, 1926; three children.

In 1929 Mrs. Snow was made editor of American *Vogue.* Then in 1932 she went as fashion editor to the rival magazine, *Harper's Bazaar,* sending shock waves through the fashion world. Condé Nast, *Vogue's* publisher, never spoke to her again. She remained with *Bazaar* as fashion editor, then as editor, until 1957, when she became chairman of the editorial board. Her successor was Nancy White, her niece and godchild.

Tiny, chic, dressed in clothes from the Paris couture, Mrs. Snow was a woman of wit and intelligence, of strong views expressed frankly and with passion. CHRISTIAN DIOR spoke of her "marvelous feeling for what is fashion today and what will be fashion tomorrow," and like a high priestess of fashion she espoused each change as it appeared. She discovered BALENCIAGA and promoted him indefatigably; was a loyal and powerful champion of the talented, demanding their best and receiving their finest efforts. After World War II, she took a leading role in helping the French and Italian textile and fashion industries get back on their feet.

As a major fashion presence and forceful personality, legends about her abound. Christian Dior delayed openings until she arrived; even when she dozed off at showings her eyes would snap open when a winner appeared; she is said to have had total ocular recall.

Mrs. Snow never completely lost her Irish accent nor her attachment to the country of her birth. She and her husband bought a place in County Mayo in 1957, later sold when the climate proved unhealthy for him. She worked there and in New York on her

51

memoirs, written in collaboration with Mary Louise Aswell, for eleven years fiction editor at *Bazaar*. Even after she no longer had official connections, and despite precarious health, she continued to go to Paris twice yearly for the collections.

Vionnet, Madeleine

(French couturière)

BORN: Aubervilliers, France, 1876.
DIED: Paris, France, 2 March 1975.

AWARDS:
1929—Chevalier Légion d'Honneur

Beaded and Embroidered Dresses

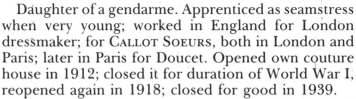

Daughter of a gendarme. Apprenticed as seamstress when very young; worked in England for London dressmaker; for CALLOT SOEURS, both in London and Paris; later in Paris for Doucet. Opened own couture house in 1912; closed it for duration of World War I, reopened again in 1918; closed for good in 1939.

Even while still working for others, Vionnet had advanced ideas not always acceptable to conservative clients. She eliminated high, boned collars from dresses and blouses, and along with POIRET, abolished corsets. She is, indisputably, a towering figure of twentieth century couture, considered one of its greatest technicians. She invented the modern use of the bias cut, producing dresses so supple they could, without the aid of placket openings, be slipped on over the head to fall back into shape on the body, eliminating the need for hooks, eyes, or fastenings of any kind. To gain even more suppleness, seams were often stitched with fagotting.

She did not sketch, working directly on the figure to drape, cut, pin. For this purpose she used a small-scaled wooden mannequin with articulated joints; designs were later translated into full-size toiles, then into the final material. While many reasons for her use of this method have been postulated, the most probable seems to be convenience; it is doubtful she could have achieved her effects as economically or with as little physical effort by any other means.

Vionnet still influences us. Her bias technique, her cowl and halter necklines, her use of pleating, are part of the designer's vocabulary today. She introduced crêpe de Chine as a fabric suitable for fashion when it had previously been confined to linings; transformed Greek and medieval inspirations into completely modern clothes, graceful and sensuous, in silk, organdy,

1934

1912

1913

1912

1913

1913

1918–19

1920

chiffon, velvet, clinging lamé; made considerable use
of handkerchief hems.

Many designers trained with her. Her assistant for
years was Marcelle Chaumont, who later opened her
own house; others included Mad Maltezos of the
House of Mad Carpentier, and Jacques Griffe.

Herself a person of complete integrity, Vionnet was
the implacable enemy of copyists and style pirates, her
motto was, "To copy is to steal."

Vreeland, Diana (born Diana Dalziel) _____

(Fashion editor and museum consultant)

BORN: Paris, France, 1906.

AWARDS:
  1970—French Order of Merit
  1976—French Legion of Honor
  1976—Dorothy Shaver "Rose" Award from Lord & Taylor
  1977—Honorary Doctor of Fine Arts Degree from Parsons School of Design

PUBLICATIONS:
  Diana Vreeland with Irving Penn. *Inventive Paris Design: 1910, 1929, 1930.*

Diana Vreeland with Bill Blass, 1979

Daughter of English father, American mother. Came to United States at outbreak of World War I. In 1924 married Thomas Reed Vreeland, who died in 1967; two sons. Naturalized American citizen.

Lived in Albany, New York, 1924–1928, in London until 1937 when husband's job brought them back to New York. Exposed from childhood to the world of fashion and to extraordinary people and events—Diaghilev, Nijinsky, Ida Rubinstein, Vernon and Irene Castle were guests in her parents' apartment—she remembers being sent to London in 1911 for coronation of George V and that Buffalo Bill gave ponies to her and her sister and taught them to ride.

Fashion career began in 1937 when, at CARMEL SNOW's request, she went to work for *Harper's Bazaar,* first writing her "Why Don't You" column which quickly became a byword for such suggestions as, "Why Don't You . . . rinse your blond child's hair in dead champagne to keep it gold as they do in France . . . ?" Became the fashion editor after six months, working closely with Mrs. Snow and art director Alexey Brodovitch to make *Bazaar* the exciting, influential publication it was. Left magazine in 1962; went to *Vogue* the same year as associate editor, then editor-in-chief, a post she held until 1971. Since 1971 has been consulting editor at *Vogue,* and also a consultant to the Costume Institute of the Metropolitan Museum of Art, instituting a series of outstanding exhibitions on such subjects as "BALENCIAGA," "American Women of Style," "The Glory of Russian Costume," "Vanity Fair," among others.

Mrs. Vreeland, who felt like an ugly duckling as a child, has created herself as an elegant, completely individual woman with a strong personal style: short, jet-black hair, bright red lips, heavily rouged cheeks. She dresses in simple "uniforms" such as sweaters and skirts for day and small dinners, appearing for big evenings in dramatic gowns from favorite designers—HALSTON, MADAME GRÈS, and GIVENCHY. Her conversational style is as original as her appearance and quite inimitable; at *Vogue* the Vreeland memos were cherished and passed around among the magazine's staffers.

As an editor, she not only reported fashion but promoted it vigorously, showing something she believed in repeatedly until it took hold. For over three decades she has been a powerful influence on the American fashion consciousness, with perhaps her greatest achievement her ability to understand the era of the 1960s with all its upheavals.

On leaving *Vogue,* she began an entirely new career, bringing to it her sense of drama, her immense energy and above all, her unquenchable enthusiasm for the unique and the beautiful. When asked the secret of her success she credited her conscientiousness and thoroughness, an inability to take short cuts.

Worth, Charles Frederick

(French couturier)

BORN: Bourne, Lincolnshire, England, 13 November 1826.
DIED: Paris, France, 10 March 1895.

Charles Frederick Worth, about 1864

Started work at 11 years, worked for a number of London drapers, eventually becoming sales clerk. Went to Paris in 1845 and took job with Maison Gagelin, dealers in fabrics, shawls, mantles. Persuaded them to open department of made-up dress models which he designed. Was first to present designs on live mannequins, in the beginning using his young French wife as a model. In 1858 opened own couture house on rue de la Paix, "Worth et Bobergh," with financial backing of Otto Bobergh. Closed 1870–1871 during Franco-Prussian War. In 1874 established Maison Worth, a fashion leader for fifty years.

Worth was court dressmaker to Empress Eugénie of France and to Empress Elizabeth of Austria; dressed ladies of European courts and society women of Europe and America. A virtual fashion dictator, he required his customers, except for Eugénie and her court, to come to him instead of attending them in their homes as had been the custom. Was widely copied, had a keen business sense, was first couturier to sell models to be copied in England and America. Enjoyed his success and lived in the grand manner.

His designs were known for their opulence and lavish use of materials, elaborate ornamentation with frills, ribbons, lace. He promoted use of French-made textiles; is held responsible for the collapsible steel frame for crinolines and for abolishing crinolines in 1867. Whether he actually invented it or not, he certainly exploited the crinoline to the utmost as it reached its most extravagant dimensions during the

Second Empire, disappearing when the Empire collapsed. Worth is said to have invented the princess-style dress; court mantles hung from the shoulders; the ancestor of the tailor-made suit; a puffed tunic called Polonaise; to have been inspired by paintings of Van Dyck, Gainsborough, and Velasquez.

House of Worth continued after his death under the leadership of his sons, Jean Philippe and Gaston, and then of his grandsons until sold in 1946. A London wholesale house now uses the name. Parfums Worth was established in 1900 and continues in Paris under great-grandson, Roger Worth.

One of Worth's sketches

2

FOREIGN DESIGNERS

Amies, Hardy
Andrévie, France
Armani, Giorgio
Aujard, Christian
Balmain, Pierre
Beretta, Anne-Marie
Bohan, Marc
Cacharel, Jean
Camerino, Guiliana
Cardin, Pierre
Cartmell, Adrian
Castelbajac, Jean-Charles de
Courrèges, André
Crahay, Jules-François
de Luca, Jean-Claude
Dorothée Bis
Fendi
Galitzine, Princess Irene
Givenchy, Hubert de
Grès, Alix
Guibourgé, Philippe
Hechter, Daniel
Kenzo
Khanh, Emmanuelle

Lagerfeld, Karl
Laroche, Guy
Laug, André
Mandelli, Mariuccia
Missoni, Rosita and Ottavio
Montana, Claude
Mori, Hanae
Mugler, Thierry
Muir, Jean
Oliver, André
Pipart, Gérard
Porter, Thea
Pucci, Emilio
Rabanne, Paco
Rhodes, Zandra
Rykiel, Sonia
Saint Laurent, Yves
Schoen, Mila
Thomass, Chantal
Ungaro, Emanuel
Valentino
Venet, Philippe
Versace, Gianni

Amies, Hardy (Edwin)

(British designer)

BORN: Maida Vale, London, England, 17 July 1909.

PUBLICATIONS:
Just So Far. St. James Place, London: Collins, 1954.
ABC of Men's Fashion. London: Newnes, 1964.

Educated Brentwood School; studied language in France and Germany, 1927–1930. Trainee at W. & T. Avery, Ltd., Birmingham, 1930–1934. Designer and managing director of Lachasse, London couture house, 1934–1939. Served in British Army Intelligence Corps 1939–1945, gained rank of lieutenant colonel; head of Special Forces Commission to Belgium, 1944; designed for House of WORTH on limited basis while in the service.

Founded dressmaking business, 1946; opened Hardy Amies Boutique, 1950. Dressmaker by Appointment to HM the Queen. Began designing men's wear in 1959 and this quickly became a major interest. Design consultant to J. Hepworth, English tailoring chain, in 1960 and subsequently to manufacturers in United States, Canada, New Zealand, Japan, South Africa.

Amies specialized from the beginning in tailored suits and coats, cocktail and evening dresses. He has been considered quite forward-looking in his breezy, contemporary clothes, such as pantsuits for women, wide yachting pants, casual classics.

He continues to operate his women's couture and ready-to-wear business, Hardy Amies, Ltd., acquired in 1973 by Debenham's, an English retail chain. Licensing agreements cover shirts, ties, shoes, as well as suits, sport coats, outerwear.

Andrévie, France

(French ready-to-wear designer)

One of young "new wave" designers. Began career in 1971 as a fashion stylist for a Brussels firm Laurent-Vicci; opened first shop in 1976 in St. Tropez, then a Paris boutique on the Place des Victoires. First collection appeared October 1976; international recognition came with second showing in March 1977.

Andrévie's designs reflect her feminist beliefs: she feels that clothes should be comfortable and stylish—and should last. She is noted for her sense of color and texture, her use of excellent fabrics, has been praised for her suits and pants.

Armani, Giorgio

(Italian ready-to-wear designer for men and women)

BORN: Emilia-Romagna, Italy, 1936.

AWARDS:
1979—Neiman-Marcus Award

Studied medicine; was assistant buyer of men's clothing for a prominent Italian department store; worked at Cerutti eight years as designer; free-lanced for many Italian manufacturers before opening own business in Milan in 1975.

First made a name with tailoring, especially blazers. Emphasis is on fine quality, easy-to-wear investment clothing at high-level prices. When doing a collection, color and fabric are primary considerations, cut comes second. Likes no-color colors such as taupe, beige, black.

Armani is very serious about his work, which leaves little time for anything else. Loves tennis; his main entertainment consists of dinners with friends at restaurants or at home.

1978

Aujard, Christian

*(French ready-to-wear
manufacturer)*

BORN: Brittany, France,
1945.
DIED: Paris, France,
8 March 1977.

Married; two children. Began as a cod fisherman; became stock clerk in apparel industry; after four years' experience, the last of which was as financial manager for a ready-to-wear firm, went into business for himself in 1968 with his wife, Michele, as chief designer. Started on a shoestring, firm grew and prospered, in Japan and the United States as well as in France. Fatally injured in a fall from a horse; business carried on by his widow.

Aujard makes tasteful, elegant clothes at moderate to better prices—women's ready-to-wear with a sportswear flavor, men's wear, and knits. They are carried in fine stores and in free-standing boutiques, including one opened in New York City in 1978.

Balmain, Pierre

(French couturier)

BORN: Aix-les-Bains, France,
18 May 1914.

AWARDS:
1955—Neiman-Marcus
Award
PUBLICATIONS:
My Years and Seasons
(autobiography). London:
Cassell & Co. Ltd., 1964.

Only child of wholesale merchant. While studying architecture at École des Beaux Arts in Paris in 1934, sketched dresses for his own amusement. Took sketches to CAPTAIN MOLYNEUX, who allowed him to work at designing in afternoons, continuing architectural studies in mornings, finally advised him to devote himself to dress design and gave him a job. Remained with Molyneux until called into army in 1939; was sent to native Savoie; returned to Paris after capitulation in 1940 to work for LUCIEN LELONG (Christian Dior joined the staff about the same time). Left Lelong in 1945 to establish his own house on rue François Ier. Opened New York ready-to-wear operation in 1951, designing special collections for the United States. Has also designed for theater and films.

Balmain takes credit for beginning the New Look; others divide it between him, DIOR, FATH and BALENCIAGA. He drew in the figure at the waist, accentuated femininity with a high bust, rounded hips, long, full skirts. Introduced tubular silhouette, still long, in 1948. Boutiques were added for men and women; the Balmain name appears on perfume, jewelry, luggage. In 1978 a Balmain dress was included in the wedding trousseau of Princess Caroline of Monaco.

Balmain dislikes fussiness, basing designs on simplicity, wearability, freedom of movement; his clothes are geared to modern living; his collections are noted for effervescent touches of wit. His philosophy: couture offers more than a seasonal change of silhouette, it expresses an ideal of elegance and refinement that follows the changing patterns of life.

Fond of travel and sports—skiing, swimming, sailing, riding.

1954

Beretta, Anne-Marie

(French ready-to-wear designer)

Works with sculptural shapes; in late 1970s was one of first to pick up the exaggerated shoulder. Strongest in coats; rubberized and ciré raincoats are a signature. Does clothes for Ramosport, leathers for MacDouglas.

Bohan, Marc

(French couturier)

BORN: Paris, France,
22 August 1926.

Mother was a milliner and encouraged his early interest in sketching and fashion. From 1945 to 1953, Bohan was assistant to ROBERT PIGUET and worked with CAPTAIN MOLYNEUX and MADELEINE DE RAUCH. Left de Rauch when not given co-designer recognition; opened couture salon in 1953, closed after one season because of inadequate financing. In 1954 became head designer at JEAN PATOU, stayed four years then left to free lance; spent three months in New York where he designed for Originala, learned much about American garment industry and began to acquire English.

In August 1958, Bohan was asked to design CHRISTIAN DIOR collections for the London, New York and South American branches; was chosen to design January collection when SAINT LAURENT was drafted into the army in September 1960. Since then he has been chief designer and artistic director of Christian Dior, now responsible for both the couture and the bou-

1978

tique ready-to-wear, as well as accessories and men's wear, bed linens for Wamsutta. He also does costumes for theater and film productions.

He is noted for refined and romantic clothes that are very wearable and carry on the Dior tradition of beautiful fabrics and exquisite workmanship. His sense of flattering color, his use of soft prints, such details as ruffles, pleats and embroidery, have made Dior among the most commercially successful houses of the couture. He feels that elegance consists of the proper adaptation of a way of dressing to the place, the atmosphere and the circumstances.

Bohan responds to beauty wherever he finds it, appreciates paintings, sculpture, photography, opera and ballet. He collects antiques; likes to vacation away from crowds, often at the seashore.

Cacharel, Jean

(French ready-to-wear designer and manufacturer)

BORN: 1932.

Studied men's tailoring; decided women's clothes offered more possibilities and went to work as designer-tailor in a small ready-to-wear shop for women. Soon opened his own shop and started making shirts; EMMANUELLE KHANH designed five collections for him. In 1961 brought back Bermuda shorts and printed shirts from the Caribbean, adapting them into culotte skirts and a flower-printed, close-to-the-body shirt which quickly became a status symbol. In 1966 hired Corinne Grandval (now Corinne Sarut), a young Beaux Arts student, to help him. She not only designs the ready-to-wear but also the characteristic prints.

The name Cacharel is synonymous with soft, sporty, classic separates in the better price range; he also produces very soft, very pretty silk dresses; in 1978 added jeans and in Europe, a perfume. Men's wear includes sweaters, shirts, pants, ties, sport jackets; there is also a children's collection; licenses cover scarves, bed linens, home sewing fabrics, McCall patterns. The clothes are designed in Paris, manufactured in the Maine region of France where Cacharel grew up and now has a country house. Mallory is the American distributor.

Camerino, Giuliana (Roberta di Camarino)

(Italian designer)

AWARDS:
1956—Neiman-Marcus
Award

Began designing and making handbags in Switzerland during World War II when she, her banker husband and infant son were refugees. Returned to Venice in 1945 and with husband established firm, "Roberta," named for her favorite movie. Daughter born a year later and also named Roberta. Business began with one employee, now has over two hundred and engages the services of more than three thousand free-lance artisans. Giuliana took over direction of company after death of her husband, aided by her daughter in charge of production, and by architect son, who has designed many of her boutiques. Designs are carried in her own stores, thirty-eight in Europe's major cities, and by fine specialty stores in the United States.

The Roberta name was established with beautiful and original handbags, especially the striped velvet satchels and pouches with carved motifs, and the exceptional leathers. The velvets are still woven and cut by hand in the ancient, time-consuming manner; the frames, handles and locks are produced in Camarino's own factories. She operates a tannery for her leathers, a fabric-printing plant, factories producing clothes and umbrellas. She has been praised by Stanley Marcus for her creativity and constant flow of new ideas. Her business now includes ready-to-wear, knitted fashions, furs, raincoats, luggage, umbrellas, men's ties and leathers, scarves, fragrances for women and men, all in the luxury classification. Her ready-to-wear features simplified, wearable shapes in fine fabrics, bold prints of her own design.

Cardin, Pierre

(French couturier)

BORN: Venice, Italy,
2 July 1922.

Grew up in St. Etienne, France. Studied architecture at parents' urging; at the age of 17 left for Vichy and began working as tailor; worked with French Red Cross in administrative post. Arrived in Paris at end of World War II; worked for PAQUIN. Executed costume designs based on sketches of Christian Bérard for Jean Cocteau's film, *La Belle et la Bête*. Introduced by Cocteau to DIOR where he headed coat and suit workroom in 1947.

First showing in his own house came in 1950. In 1954 established two boutiques, "Adam" for men, selling ties, waistcoats, sweaters, and "Eve" for women. Became prominent in 1957 with innovative designs for women; started men's wear in 1958; added children's apparel in 1968.

Considered one of the most creative, intellectual, avant-garde couturiers of the 1950s and 1960s; showed the first nude look in 1966; metal body jewelry; unisex astronaut suits; helmets; batwing jumpsuits; tunics over tights. His work in the late 1970s retains the precise lines characteristic of his tailoring background; well-cut suits and coats; evening dresses in brilliant satins, often with uneven hemlines.

Prolific and protean, Cardin expands his interests in every direction. In 1970 he remodeled the "Théâtre des Ambassadeurs" and renamed it "L'Espace Pierre Cardin," with a restaurant, a movie house for experimental work, exposition halls, meeting rooms. His name appears on jewelry, watches, eyeglass frames, bed linens, luggage, accessories; on men's apparel, furnishings, jewelry, small leather goods, shoes, toiletries. A wig collection appeared in 1972. In 1979, he entered into a trade agreement with the Peoples Republic of China.

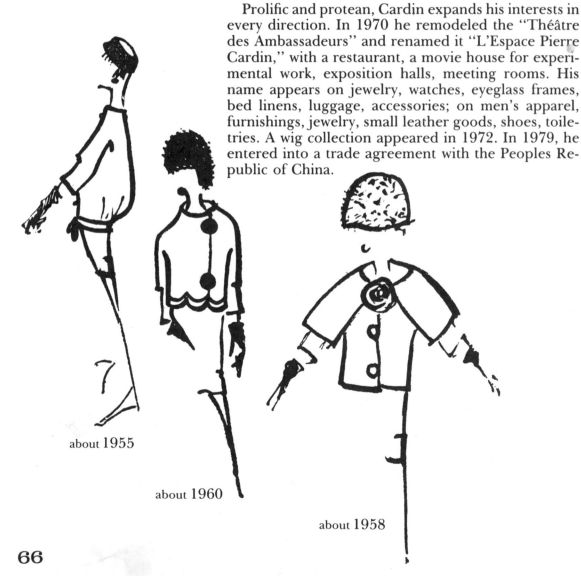

about 1955

about 1960

about 1958

66

Cartmell, Adrian

(English designer)

Born: 1949.

Studied fashion six years at Birmingham Polytechnic; spent two years in Leicester studying knitwear. Designed for Manson, 1970–1978, beginning with sweaters and shirts and progressing to a full wardrobe. Formed his own firm in fall 1978.

Cartmell is credited with an excellent eye for line and proportion, a terrific color sense, total professionalism. He makes sophisticated clothes—coats, suits, dresses—in subtle shapes, wearable interpretations of current trends, well made in excellent fabrics. He feels the purpose of fashion is "to turn ugly ducklings into swans."

For relaxation, he likes dancing and partying.

Castelbajac, Jean-Charles de

(French designer)

Part of the ready-to-wear movement which burgeoned in France in the 1960s and came into full flower in the 1970s. Best known for the fashion flair he gives to survival looks: blanket plaids, canvas, quilting; rugged coats and sportswear for both women and men.

Courrèges, André

(French couturière)

Born: Pau, in the Basque region, France, 9 March 1923.

Studied civil engineering then switched to study of textiles and fashion design; first in Pau, later in Paris. First job was with Jeanne Lafaurie; worked for BALENCIAGA, 1952–1960.

Opened own Paris house in August 1961. Wife, Coqueline, who had spent three years with Balenciaga, helped with the designing, choosing the mannequins, staging the shows. Together they designed, cut, sewed and presented their first collection in a small apartment in the avenue Kleber.

Courrèges emerged as a superb tailor. His early clothes had an architectural quality similar to Balenciaga's. Using woolens with considerable body, he cut his coats and suits with a triangular flare which disguised many figure defects, the balanced, classical silhouettes defined by crisp welt seaming. His aim was to make functional, modern clothes. He made an impact with all-white collections; tunics over narrow pants that were flared and cut at a slant at the bottom; squared-off dresses ending above the knee; sequined suspender dresses in checks or broad stripes; short white baby boots; his use of industrial zippers; zany accessories such as sunglasses with slit "tennis ball" lenses.

In 1965 sold business to L'Oréal and for a year did only custom work for private clients. Returned to design in 1967 with see-through dresses; cosmonaut suits and knitted "cat" suits; a naked look in sheer fabrics and big oval cutouts, flowers appliquéd on the body; knee socks. Was labeled "couturier of the space age."

In the 1970s the Courrèges designs have been more feminine, with an ingenue flavor underlined by ruffles, softer colors, softer fabrics. There are Courrèges accessories, luggage, perfumes, men's wear. He has

created uniforms for the 1972 Olympic Games at Munich and for airline flight attendants. Ready-to-wear boutiques in the United States and other countries carry everything from sports separates to accessories to his "Couture Future" de luxe ready-to-wear.

Crahay, Jules-François ————————

(French designer)

BORN: Liege, Belgium, 1918.

AWARDS:
1962—Neiman-Marcus Award

Began fashion career in 1951 as salesperson for Jane Regny. Chief designer for NINA RICCI, 1954 to 1963; head designer for House of LANVIN since 1963. During the early 1970s did a ready-to-wear collection for Arkin in New York.

Crahay was one of the first to glamorize pants for evening in pleated organdy, or silk; has developed ethnic themes such as jeweled leather gaucho pants, harem hems, peasant looks in Guatemalan cottons.

André Courrèges, 1965

de Luca, Jean-Claude

(French ready-to-wear designer)

BORN: 1948.

1978

Studied law and passed first bar exams before deciding against law as a career. Introduced to GIVENCHY, 1971; worked for him for over a year studying cut, design, and fabrics. In 1976 began designing under his own name.

De Luca aims at glamour, humor and poetry in his clothes; thinks of what a woman needs for a modern situation then works to supply it. He feels that her requirements for day and night are almost the same, prefers to do evening clothes like sport pieces in materials such as satin or lamé, sometimes quilted or printed, with exaggerated accessories for wit.

Dorothée Bis

(French knitwear house)

French knitwear house which began in the 1960s as a chain of trend-setting Paris boutiques, managed by Jacqueline Jacobson, designer-buyer, and her husband Elie. The Jacobsons are among the pioneers of French ready-to-wear. They began in the fur business, went into skirts, then into knits. They are known for intarsia knits in imaginative patterns and for brilliant use of color. Collections are totally color-keyed, from knitted cap to knitted gloves to ribbed wool tights matched to shoes or boots. Clothes are widely distributed in the United States; there have been Dorothée Bis boutiques in Henri Bendel and Bloomingdale's in New York, and in other stores across the country. A life-sized rag doll slumped in a chair is the display trademark of the shops.

Fendi

(Italian fur house)

1978

Italian family firm specializing in furs, handbags, luggage, some clothes. Founded in 1918 by Adele Fendi, who died 19 March 1978 at the age of 81; built up and expanded by her with the help of five daughters, Paola, Anna, Franca, Carla and Alda, working as a team.

When Signora Fendi's husband died in 1954, her daughters, aged 14 to 24, had to help in the business. They worked with manufacturers on the handbags and persuaded fur cutters to innovate. In 1962 they hired KARL LAGERFELD to design their furs and backed him with new, unusual or forgotten pelts; they introduced color to furs. Anna, who evolved the style for their bags, looked for soft leathers to make pliable, feminine, lightweight bags; a successful summer style was made by weaving strips of binding canvas; in 1966 a plastic evening clutch was another much-copied success.

Fendi styles have glamour, but their success appears to be based on the sisters' understanding, as working women themselves, of what other women need and want. Their mother made coats out of squirrel and made them fashionable, the Fendis today still use squirrel, as well as badger, Persian lamb, fox and sundry unpedigreed furs, often several in one garment. They are noted for inventive techniques and styling, such as furs woven in strips for a fishnet effect, accordion pleats; shawls and boleros of mink petals; coats left unlined for lightness or lined in silk. And the furs are always fun. The Fendi double F initials designed by Karl Lagerfeld have become a status symbol; the sisters continue to explore new areas and their daughters, in turn, are waiting to carry on the Fendi dynasty.

Galitzine, Princess Irene

(Italian couturière)

BORN: Russia.

Raised in Rome after her family fled the Russian Revolution. Married to Silvio Medici, Italian-Brazilian industrialist. Always interested in clothes; studied art and design in Rome. Worked for FONTANA sisters for three years; opened her own import business in Rome, 1948; first show of her own designs, 1949. House declared bankrupt in 1968; Galitzine continued in fashion, designing cosmetics, furs, household linens for various companies. Her couture house has been revived and in the late 1970s she was again showing.

Galitzine became known in the 1960s for silk "palazzo" or dinner pajamas, often fringed with beads, sometimes with attached necklaces; also for at-home togas, evening suits, tunic-top dresses, evening gowns with bare backs or open sides. In the late 1970s her emphasis is on simple lines, rich fabrics, exotic prints.

Givenchy, Hubert de

(French couturier)

BORN: Beauvais, France, 20 February 1927.

Studied at École des Beaux Arts. Started in couture at age 17 with FATH; worked at PIGUET and LELONG, spent four years at SCHIAPARELLI where he designed separates, cardigan dresses and blouses for the boutique.

Opened his own house, February 1952, near BALENCIAGA whom he admired greatly and by whom he was much influenced.

He gained early recognition for his youthful separates and for the "Bettina blouse," named for the famous French model who worked with him when he first opened. This was a peasant shape with open neckline and full ruffled sleeves, made up in shirting. When Balenciaga closed his house, Givenchy took over many of the workroom people, assuming as well much of the older designer's reputation for super-refined couture. He has an extensive and conservative clientele; his clothes are noted for superb cut and workmanship, beautiful fabrics. In the late 1970s, while the day clothes remained in this framework of quiet elegance, the late-day and evening segments of the collection were exuberantly glamorous.

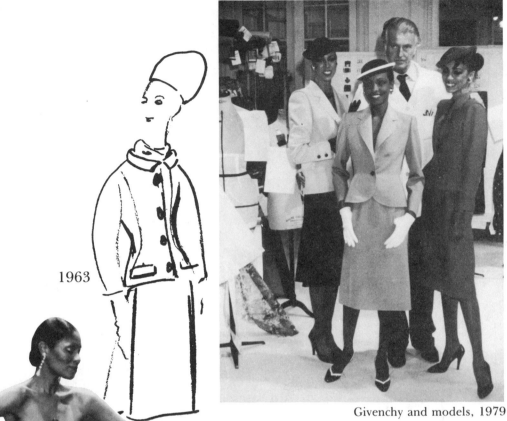

1963

Givenchy and models, 1979

1979

In addition to his couture house, one of the few truly profitable ones, Givenchy's interests include his Nouvelle Boutique ready-to-wear distributed in Europe, the United States, Japan; perfumes for women; men's toiletries; his own costume jewelry firm. Licensing commitments extend from sportswear to shirts for men and women to small leather goods, hosiery, furs, eyeglasses, home furnishings.

Givenchy's avocations include house decoration and antique collecting; he is an excellent swimmer and has become interested in boating.

Alix (born Alix Barton)

(couturière)

BORN: Paris, France,
c. 1910.

1952

1975

Married to Serge Grès, painter and sculptor; one daughter. First career choice was sculpture. Apprenticed at House of Premet; in 1931–1932 was making *toiles,* the muslin patterns of couture designs, under the name of Alix Barton. Had a salon before the war under the name of Alix, closed in 1942; reopened after the war using her married name of Grès.

Madame Grès is widely considered one of the most talented, imaginative and independent designers of the couture, ranked by many with VIONNET although very different. Her background as a sculptor shows in the way she drapes, especially her evening dresses of chiffon and the fine silk jersey called "Alix" after her use of it. These she pleats closely, molding them to the figure, always baring some portion of the midriff. A number of other themes recur in each collection: evening gowns in two colors, jersey day dresses with cowl necklines, deep-cut or dolman sleeves, kimono-shaped coats, asymmetric draping. Her perfume is named "Cabochard," which means obstinate. She has never expanded into ready-to-wear.

Small and serious, Grès is shy of publicity, goes her own way as a designer, approaching her work in the spirit of the artist she is. She has a devoted following in France, England, the United States.

In the early 1970s was president of the Chambre Syndicale de la Haute Couture.

Guibourgé, Philippe

(French designer)

While still in army, showed drawings to JACQUES FATH, later worked with him for three years, training in all departments. Simultaneously assisted with the couture collections and with the couturier's first ready-to-wear line. In 1960 went to CHRISTIAN DIOR; for twelve years collaborated on the couture collections as assistant to MARC BOHAN and was responsible for ready-to-wear collections created for England, supervised design of fashion accessories sold in the boutique. From 1967 to 1975, was responsible for Miss Dior ready-to-wear, during five of the eight years continuing to collaborate on the couture. In 1975 left Dior to become art director of Creations Chanel, the new CHANEL ready-to-wear and accessory collections.

Guibourgé has been described as "one of the nicest of the designers, without temperament, an excellent cook, a devoted son." He is very active, refreshes himself by changing activities; has a passion for furniture of the 17th and 18th centuries but also appreciates contemporary art.

Hechter, Daniel

(French ready-to-wear designer)

BORN: 1938.

Hechter started career designing for Pierre D'Alby; opened own business in 1962, first for women, then children; in 1970 presented first men's sportswear collections.

Hechter's clothes are geared to young, active people who are career-oriented and imaginative. The designs embody sportswear ease, function and dash developed as wearable, affordable, comfortable fashion. He strives for a sense of reality, a continuity of line and color from season to season so that clothes bought in one· season can be added to those from the previous one, and built on in the next.

In the late 1970s, besides his business in France, he sells in Italy and Germany and the United States; has licensing arrangements in England, Spain, Japan, Canada; has recently designed an active sportswear collection, including ski clothes. Opened a New York boutique in 1978.

He is an avid skier, has a wide spectrum of interests ranging from art to politics.

Kenzo (Kenzo Takada)

(French designer)

BORN: Japan, 1945.

Started fashion career in Tokyo designing patterns for a magazine. Arrived in Paris around 1964. Found work with a style bureau where he designed up to twenty collections a year; freelanced for many companies including Rodier. In 1970 opened his own boutique and decorated every inch with jungle patterns, named it "Jungle Jap." Clothes were an immediate success with young fashion individualists such as models.

First ready-to-wear collection was for the winter sea-

1978

son and due to lack of money was made entirely of cotton, much of it quilted. It was shown on photographic rather than regular runway mannequins and to the sound of rock music, innovations which like other Kenzo ideas were the beginning of a trend. The clothes caught on with American stores starting in 1971 and are now widely distributed in the United States. In addition to sweaters, knits, dresses, coats, suits, Kenzo designs for Butterick Patterns and has expanded into men's wear. In the late 1970s planned a perfume and licensing arrangements, including bed linens.

Kenzo is considered by his peers to be one of the most prophetic designers in ready-to-wear, a prolific originator of fresh ideas, widely copied, extremely salable.

Khanh, Emmanuelle

(French designer)

Born: Plain, France, c. 1938.

Married to Vietnamese engineer, Nyuen Manh (Quasar) Khanh. Began in fashion as mannequin for BALENCIAGA and GIVENCHY; is credited with starting the young fashion movement in France in 1963 when, rebelling against the couture, she commenced designing inexpensive ready-to-wear. Clothes were sold in boutiques in Paris and London, then in the United States where she has also designed men's fashions for Puritan.

Khanh first became known for "the Droop," a very slim, soft, close-to-the-body dress and for other dresses with a lanky 1930s feeling; and for such details as dogs' ear collars, droopy lapels on long fitted jackets, dangling cuff-link fastenings, half-moon money-bag pockets. Altogether her work reflected an individual approach symbolic of the 1960s. In the late 1970s she was still producing soft and imaginative clothes.

agerfeld, Karl

(French designer)

BORN: Hamburg, Germany, 1939.

Son of Swedish father, German mother. Arrived in Paris at age 14, already with the ambition to become a clothes designer. Won first award for dress design in 1955, meanwhile continuing his education by reading, informal study, extensive travel.

Lagerfeld is designer for the House of Chloé, producing ready-to-wear with couture attributes, original, exquisite, expensive. He is considered one of the most individual, most prophetic designers, likes to remove clothes from their usual contexts so they acquire freshness; at various times has showed tennis shoes

1979

with crêpe de Chine dresses, used elaborate embroidery on cottons instead of on silks, made dresses that can be worn upside down. After specializing in fluid, seamless, layered looks, made a dramatic switch in his late 1970s collection with a move to more structure, exaggerated shoulders, drastically shortened skirts.

In addition to his Chloé collections, he designs his own fabrics, is, or has been, involved with furs, gloves; shoes for Charles Jourdan; sweaters for Ballantyne; furs for FENDI. Two fragrances, "Chloé" for women, "Lagerfeld" for men.

Lagerfeld puts as much style into his private life as into his collections. He has developed a passion for the 18th century and in 1976 auctioned off his notable collection of Art Deco furnishings; in 1977 took an apartment in an 18th-century Paris mansion. He loves books, movies, music from Mozart to Stravinsky to the Beatles.

Laroche, Guy

(French couturier)

BORN: La Rochelle (near Bordeaux), France, c. 1923.

Family in business of raising cattle. No formal design training; worked briefly in hairdressing and millinery. Spent three years in United States with several Seventh Avenue manufacturers; worked eight years with JEAN DESSÈS. Laroche established his own couture house in Paris with first collection for fall 1957, mostly coats and suits; dresses followed.

In the beginning his designs were influenced by BALENCIAGA, then developed into a younger, gayer look. Expanded in 1961, opened a boutique, started a ready-to-wear line. Introduced men's wear and a boutique for men, 1966; makeup and fragrance, 1967; men's toiletries, 1972, the same year he opened a factory in Dieppe; added a new perfume, "J'ai Osé," 1978. There are boutiques for men and women in many countries; licensing includes lingerie, scarves, hats, bags, jewelry, belts, shoes, shirts, ties.

Laroche is recognized as a creative designer and a shrewd businessman, with a following among entertainment personalities and socialites.

Laug, André

(French designer working in Italy)

BORN: Alsace, France,
1932.

Worked briefly for NINA RICCI and ANDRÉ COUR-
RÈGES; designed for ANTONELLI for five years. Has
couture house in Rome; shows ready-to-wear in Milan.

Makes both couture and deluxe ready-to-wear.
Clothes are refined in cut and attitude, beautifully
made. He interprets young ideas for his conservative
international clientele.

Mandelli, Mariuccia

(Italian ready-to-wear designer)

BORN: 1933.

Designer for Krizia, which she runs with husband,
Aldo Pinto, and for less expensive knit label, Rizia-
maglia. One of Italy's wittiest, most original designers;
clothes are upbeat, youthful, sophisticated, presented
with perfectly chosen accessories.

Missoni, Rosita and Ottavio

*(Italian knitwear designers and
manufacturers)*

AWARDS:
  1973—Neiman-Marcus
    Award

Married April 1953; three children. Couple met at
1948 London Olympics where Ottavio (Tai) was com-
peting as a member of the Italian track team. He was
a manufacturer of athletes' sweat suits (his styles had
been accepted as part of the official Olympic uniform)
and she was studying languages at a girls' college in
Hempstead. She also worked for her parents in their
small manufacturing company.

The Missonis knew when they married that they
wanted to do something together but they did not
start right off as fashion leaders. They began their
business in 1953 with four knitting machines. Their
first designs were not sold under their own label but
appeared anonymously in department stores or in
boutiques under the names of other designers. Moving toward more adventurous styling, they hired Paris
designers—first EMMANUELLE KHANH and later, Chris-
tiane Bailly. After a few seasons Rosita took over the
designing herself.

At a time when knits were considered basics, Ot-

1978

tavio's startling geometric and abstract patterns
created a furor, as did the first Missoni showing in
Florence in 1967. Rosita had the models remove their
bras so they would not show through the thin knits
and the stage lighting caused the clothes to look transparent. The result was a scandal in the Italian press.
The Missonis were not invited back to Florence and
decided to show closer to home in Milan.

Now very much an international status symbol, the
Missoni knit is highly recognizable by virtue of its col-
oring and texture. The collections are a joint effort.
Ottavio creates the distinctive patterns and stitches
and works out the colorings then submits them to
Rosita; they then work together on the line. She does

not sketch but with an assistant drapes directly on the model. Shapes are kept simple to set off the knit designs, each collection is built around a few classics—pants, skirts, long cardigan jackets, sweaters, capes, dresses. Production is limited and the clothes are expensive. In addition to the women's styles there are a limited number of designs for men and children. In 1974 the patterns were licensed to Fieldcrest for bed and bath linens.

The Missonis live in considerable style but without pomp in a house they built in Sumirago, a small village in the Lombardy hills of northern Italy. Their children are: Vittorio, born in 1955 and now in the family business, Luca, born in 1957, and Angela, born in 1959.

In April 1978, to celebrate the 25th anniversary of their business and their marriage, they gave a party at an art gallery to show their fall line. Instead of the usual runway presentation, live mannequins in the new styles posed next to dummies displaying designs from previous years, arranged without regard to chronological order. Except for the mini skirts and hot pants it was nearly impossible to date them. Examples of the knit patterns were framed and hung on the wall along with blowups of photographs from fashion magazines. It was an effective demonstration of the timeless character of their designs.

Montana, Claude

(French designer)

BORN: 1949.

Began designing in 1971 on a trip to London when, to make money, he concocted papier-mâché jewelry encrusted with rhinestones. These were featured in fashion magazines and earned him enough money to stay in London for a year. He returned to Paris and after a year of doing little, went to work for MacDouglas, a French leather firm.

Montana is prominent among the young French ready-to-wear designers of the late 1970s. He works in bold, well-defined shapes—largely suits, coats, jackets, pants—much of the time in the soft, spongy leather called cuir de plongée. His clothes are manufactured in Spain by Ferrer y Sentis, sold in fine United States' stores as well as in Paris, Italy, Germany, Eng-

1979

land. Under license, they are made and distributed in Japan.

His personal living style is simple—jeans, boots, windbreakers of nylon or leather are his preferred dress. Among French ready-to-wear designers he greatly admires KENZO; considers MADAME GRÈS the epitome of haute couture.

ori, Hanae

(Japanese couturière)

BORN: Tokyo, Japan,
8 January 1926.

AWARDS:
1973—Neiman-Marcus
Award

Graduated Tokyo Christian Women's College with a degree in Japanese literature. Married to Ken Mori, who worked in the textile industry; two sons. After her marriage, which was a love match, and a period as a housewife, she went to school to learn sewing, sketching, designing, then opened a small boutique in the Shinjuku section of Tokyo. Her clothes attracted the attention of the burgeoning Japanese movie industry and she designed costumes for innumerable films. In 1955 she opened her first shop on the Ginza, Tokyo's famous shopping street; went on to develop a multi-million dollar international business. Her husband helps manage the company; her older son, Akira, manages the New York business from their 79th Street townhouse.

Mori makes extensive use of her Japanese background both in her fabrics—woven, printed and dyed especially for her—and in the shapes of the clothes themselves. To evoke the mood of Japan's Edo period she has utilized the vivid colors and bold linear patterns of Hiroshige prints; butterflies and flowers, the Japanese symbols of femininity, show up frequently in her prints; she has adapted traditional kimono materials and shapes for her cocktail and evening dresses, the area in which she is best known, while also working in more conventional Western modes.

Hanae Mori brought her couture collection to Paris in January 1977 and continues to show there each season; her ready-to-wear is sold at fine stores throughout the world; her boutiques sell her scarves, bags, shoes, soft sportswear, innerwear, and towels in many countries. Her fabric designs are licensed for bed and bath linens; she designed skiwear for the Sapporo Winter Olympic Games in 1972; in June 1978 she opened a building in Tokyo which houses boutiques, the couture operation and her business offices.

Mugler, Thierry

(French ready-to-wear designer)

One of the young design contingent prominent in the late 1970s. Known for high-priced separates and dresses with a broad-shouldered, defined-waistline silhouette, an architectural feeling. As shown on the runway, clothes appear aggressive and tough; close up, they prove to be simple, body-fitted, not overly detailed. They have sold well in the United States.

Muir, Jean

(English designer)

BORN: London, England,
c. 1933.

AWARDS:
1967, 1968, 1974, 1976—
Maison Blanche "Rex"
Award, New Orleans
1973—Fellow of the Royal
Society of Arts
1973—Neiman-Marcus
Award

Of Scottish descent. Started as sketcher at Liberty; joined Jaeger, and soon became responsible for the designs of major dress and knitwear collections. Designer for Jane and Jane, 1962. Established Jean Muir, Inc. and opened Jean Muir Shop at Henri Bendel, New York in 1967. Married to Harry Leuckert, formerly an actor, now her business manager; one daughter.

Muir is one of the new breed of anti-couture, anti-establishment designers who came up in the late 1950s and early 1960s. She has created a signature look in gentle, pretty clothes of the luxury investment category, is especially admired for her leathers which are completely soft and feminine. She is also known for evening dresses in soft printed chiffons, for frequent use of bloomers and knickers and for excellent coats. Geraldine Stutz of Henri Bendel has called her "the leather lady of the Western world."

1975

Oliver, André

(French designer)

BORN: Toulouse, France, 1932.

Attended the École des Beaux Arts. In 1952 went to work for PIERRE CARDIN; became designer of both the men's and women's ready-to-wear collections. Since October 1977, president of André Oliver, Inc., New York, a fine men's wear shop. He continues to be associated as designer with Cardin.

Oliver lives and works in New York a good part of the year; is a collector of art and antiques.

Pipart, Gérard

(French designer)

BORN: 1933.

Started in fashion at 16 selling sketches to PIERRE BALMAIN, for whom he worked briefly, and to JACQUES FATH, with whom he stayed six months. Sketched for GIVENCHY, went with MARC BOHAN during the short time he had his own house. Did two-year army service in Tunisia.

Came back from the army and free-lanced in ready-to-wear; did a single unsuccessful couture collection in 1963. Returned to ready-to-wear with great success for firms on the Côte d'Azur, others in Italy and London, including Germaine et Jane, Jean Baillie-Hemcey, Chloé. In 1963 succeeded JULES-FRANCOIS CRAHAY as chief designer at NINA RICCI, has remained there ever since doing both the couture and Mademoiselle Ricci boutique collections.

Pipart has never learned to cut or sew. He works from detailed sketches and makes corrections directly on the toiles. His taste is for simplicity, he avoids showiness and fussy details, detests gimmicks. Described as a happy, gentle man of great charm, he is known for young, spirited clothes, has been compared to Jacques Fath, whom he considers "the most wonderful personality I ever knew or saw." Among other designers, he greatly admires Givenchy and the late BALENCIAGA.

Porter, Thea (born Dorothea Seal)

(English designer of interiors, clothes, fabrics)

BORN: Damascus, Syria.

Daughter of French mother, English father. Lived in Lebanon and Turkey; married a British embassy official and spent time in Beirut off and on from 1950 to 1963. Returned to London in 1963 after her marriage broke up and opened an interior decorating shop in the Soho district.

As atmosphere for the shop, she imported a number of caftans of the kind worn by Middle Eastern brides, which were greatly admired by her customers. At their request, she began to reproduce the caftans in authentic fabrics and from there went on to become well known for timeless, fantasy evening dresses and pajamas in unusual materials. Her designs were strongly marked by ethnic influences from the Middle and Far East and also by periods in Western history—the Renaissance, the Victorian and Gothic eras. By the early 1970s she was focusing on the 1940s, with so-called "drippy" chiffons in her own prints, mixing several prints in a single outfit; adding men's clothes—caftans, velvet suits, printed chiffon shirts.

Porter has always worked in an off-beat, anti-couture mood. In 1968 her clothes were sold at Vidal Sassoon's London salon and in New York at Henri Bendel. She opened a New York boutique in 1971, closed it in 1972. In October 1976 she opened a couture boutique on the rue Tournon in Paris, moving her entire operation there the same year. She has continued to develop her favorite themes—dressy djellabahs, beading, sequins, hand embroidery—in couture and deluxe evening ready-to-wear. Her clothes are popular with entertainment personalities and with well-off private customers who want something different.

Pucci, Emilio
(Marchese Emilio Pucci di Barsento)

(Italian designer)

BORN: Naples, Italy.

Descendant of Italian and Russian nobility. Educated in Italy at the University of Milan; in the United States at the University of Georgia. Received M.A. degree in social science in 1937 from Reed College,

AWARDS:
1954—Neiman-Marcus
Award

Portland, Oregon; doctorate in political science in 1941 from University of Florence. Member of the Italian Olympic Ski Team in 1933 and 1934; officer of Italian Air Force during World War II; member of Italian Parliament.

In 1947 was discovered as a designer of his own ski clothes by fashion photographer Toni Frissell. The following year he designed women's ski wear for Lord & Taylor; in 1949 opened his own shop in Capri and a workshop in Florence; by 1950 had a couture house named "Emilio," boutiques in Capri, Rome, Elba, Montecatini.

While it was Pucci's classic, well-cut sportswear that first brought him notice, his brilliant signature prints in designs taken from heraldic banners became part of the status "Pucci Look" of the 1960s. His simple chemises made of thin silk jersey were favorites of the international jet set and were widely copied in cheaper jerseys.

Other design projects have included at-home robes, tights, scarves, sportswear, bathing suits. There are Pucci fragrances for women and men; he has designed lingerie and other intimate apparel for Formfit Rogers, ski clothes for White Stag, porcelain for Rosenthal, uniforms for Braniff Airlines, bath linens, rugs.

Rabanne, Paco

(French designer)

BORN: San Sebastián, Spain, 1934.

Son of BALENCIAGA's head dressmaker; family fled Spain for France in 1939 because of Spanish Civil War. Rabanne studied architecture; began designing plastic accessories.

In 1966 he made a splash with dresses of metal-linked plastic discs, plastic jewelry, and sun goggles in primary colors. He continued the linked-disc idea in fur-patch coats, leather-patch dresses, buttons laced with wire, strips of aluminum. Led with fake-suede dresses in 1970; coats of knit-and-fur; dresses of ribbons, feathers or tassels linked for suppleness. He continues to design in the late 1970s; has two successful fragrances: "Calandre" for women, "Paco" for men.

Rhodes, Zandra

(English designer)

BORN: Chatham, Kent,
England, 1942.

1978

Father was a truck driver; mother was head fitter at WORTH in Paris, following her marriage was senior lecturer at Medway College of Art. Rhodes graduated from Royal College of Art, 1966. Began career as a textile designer; set up her own print works; by 1969 was producing her own imaginative clothing designs.

A complete original, Rhodes works largely in very soft fabrics—chiffon, tulle, silk—often handscreened in her own prints: Art Deco motifs, lipsticks, teddy bears, squiggles, zigzags, teardrops, big splashy patterns. She has made news with edges finished by pinking shears; has been criticized for glamorized Punk clothes with torn holes or edges, fastened with jeweled safety pins, sleeves held on by pins or chains; has been applauded for her champagne bubble dresses drawn in at the knee with elastic, hems ending in flounces finished with uneven scallops and adorned with pearls or pompoms or braid.

Introduced Zandra Rhodes sportswear for fall 1978; designs sleepwear, textiles, sheets, rugs; pays frequent visits to the United States where her clothes are sold in such stores as Henri Bendel and Bloomingdale's.

Rhodes's personal appearance is startling, in the great English tradition of eccentricity. Her hair may be dyed in a rainbow of colors—magenta and bright green, for example—her makeup tends to the extraordinary with such effects as eyebrows drawn in one continuous arc. Unlike many of her contemporaries from 1960's "swinging London," she has continued to take risks and remains in the avant-garde.

Rykiel, Sonia

(French designer)

Started fashion career by making her own maternity dresses; continued to design clothes for friends after her son was born. Did clothes for husband's firm "Laura"; opened Sonia Rykiel boutique in 1968 in the Paris department store Galeries Lafayette, then opened her own boutique on the Left Bank.

Rykiel made her name and developed an international following in the late 1960s with liberated, unconstructed clothes: long, body-close sweaters; sheer gowns over body stockings; long, side-slit day skirts; layered knits. Has added a men's sweater line, a perfume. In the late 1970s continues in her own individualistic, personal design path.

Saint Laurent, Yves

(French couturier)

BORN: Oran, Algeria,
   1 August 1936.

AWARDS:
   1958—Neiman-Marcus
   Award

At age 18 went to Paris to study art; entered competition sponsored by the International Wool Secretariat and won a prize for his cocktail dress design; hired by CHRISTIAN DIOR, one of the judges. Worked for him until Dior's death in 1957, when Saint Laurent was chosen to succeed him as head designer. Called up for military service in 1960; after three months became ill and was discharged. Opened his own salon in January 1962. Established "Rive Gauche" boutiques for ready-to-wear in 1966; men's wear in 1974. His name and the YSL initials are found on everything from sweaters to bed linens, eyeglasses to scarves. A children's line designed in Paris and made in the United States was introduced in fall 1978.

Saint Laurent feels that his success depends on his ability to tune in on the life of the moment. From the start he has been probably the most successful interpreter of modern moods, picking up inspiration from the street and transmuting it into elegant fashion, consistently setting trends followed by the rest of the world. From early in 1970 he placed special emphasis on the ready-to-wear collections, often working out ideas that appeared later in couture. Toward the end of the 1970s, the couture became ever more refined and subtle, infinitely luxurious in its use of rich materials, handwork, embroidery, elegant with a dash

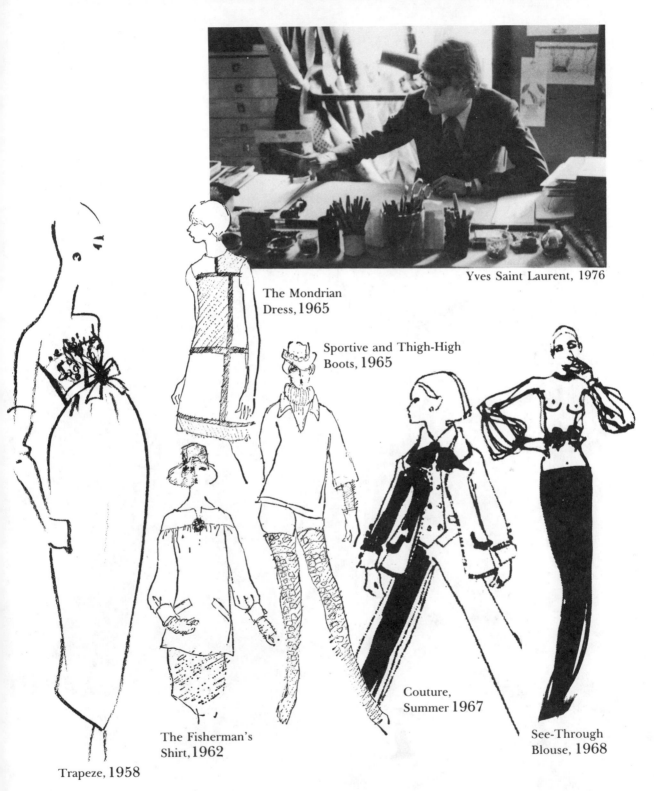

Yves Saint Laurent, 1976

The Mondrian
Dress, 1965

Sportive and Thigh-High
Boots, 1965

Couture,
Summer 1967

See-Through
Blouse, 1968

The Fisherman's
Shirt, 1962

Trapeze, 1958

91

Yves Saint Laurent

Sportive Separates, 1971

Longuette, 1970

Russian Fantasy, 1976

Couture, Summer 1979

The Evening
Tuxedo, 1978

of wit in colors and accessories. He has been called the last of the great couturiers.

Among the high points of his career have been the 1958 "Trapeze" of his first Dior collection; the pea coat and the "smoking"; city pantsuits; the see-through nude look of 1966; the rich peasants, 1976; the refined tailoring with a subtle feeling of the body beneath in spring 1978.

Schoen, Mila

(Italian couturière)

Based in Milan, shows in Rome. Established business in 1959; makes couture and deluxe ready-to-wear. Became important during the 1960s and early 1970s for beautifully cut suits and coats in double-faced fabrics and for exquisitely beaded evening dresses, sequined vests and shorts. Her clothes have evolved to a softer, more fluid look.

Thomass, Chantal

(French ready-to-wear designer)

BORN: 1947.

No formal design training; when in her teens started designing her own clothes, which her mother made up for her. Later she made clothes out of silk scarves painted by art student boy friend; in 1967 sold some of these dresses to DOROTHÉE BIS and to Le Café des Arts in Saint Tropez, where they were bought by Brigitte Bardot. Married that year to Bruce Thomass and the two started a firm called Ter et Bantine, making "very junior," rather eccentric clothes. Established Chantal Thomass firm in 1976 for a more expensive line using silk, lace, organza and chiffon for summer; angora, mohair and felt for winter. The clothes are pretty and feminine with a young, up-to-the-minute spirit.

Thomass collects clothes, shoes, jewelry, hats; is interested in Art Nouveau and spends her leisure time in auction rooms looking for furniture and paintings for her country house. She is fond of travel; enjoys meeting new people, seeing new things.

Ungaro, Emanuel _____

(French couturier)

BORN: Aix-en-Provence,
France, 13 February 1933.

AWARDS:
1969—Neiman-Marcus
Award

Of Italian parentage. After finishing school, worked for his father, a tailor, until age 22; learned to cut, sew, and fit men's clothes. Went to Paris to a small tailoring concern; decided he would rather design for women. Worked for BALENCIAGA from 1958 to 1963; spent two seasons with COURRÈGES in 1964.

Opened own business, 1965. First collections reminiscent of Courrèges with tailored coats and suits, diagonal seaming, little girl A-line dresses, blazers with shorts. Clothes were young, widely copied in the youth market. Many of his special fabrics were designed by Sonja Knapp, a German-Swiss who studied art in Zurich and who still works with him.

In the late 1970s he turned to softer fabrics, more flowing lines, mingling several different prints in a single outfit, and piling on layers. He has added ready-to-wear, has boutiques in Europe and the United States, a perfume; has done furs and men's wear; has a Japanese contract for sheets, wall coverings, curtains. First American knitwear collection appeared in fall 1978.

Valentino (Valentino Garavani) _____

(Italian couturier)

BORN: Voghera, Italy,
1932.

AWARDS:
1967—Neiman-Marcus
Award

Left high school at age 17 to go to Paris; studied at a school of design and at the École des Beaux Arts.

Between 1950 and 1958 worked five years as assistant to JEAN DESSÈS, then two years for GUY LAROCHE. Returned to Italy in 1960 and opened a couture house in Rome. First boutique for ready-to-wear opened in Milan in 1969, followed by one in Rome, then others around the world, including Japan. Began showing his ready-to-wear collections in Paris, October 1975. Other interests include men's wear; Valentino Piu for gifts and interiors; licenses for bed linens, curtain and drapery fabrics, etc.

His clothes are noted for refined simplicity and elegance—well-cut coats and suits, sophisticated sportswear, entrance-making evening dresses—always feminine and flattering. They are worn by an international roster of well-heeled and fashionable women.

Valentino lives opulently, has a villa outside Rome, places in Capri and Gstaad. In October 1978, he introduced his Valentino fragrance in France in the grand manner, sponsoring a ballet performance in Paris and after-theater parties at Maxim's and the Palace.

1979

Venet, Philippe

(French couturier)

BORN: Lyons, France, 22 May 1929.

Began to learn tailoring when he was 14. Worked at SCHIAPARELLI, 1951 to 1953; met GIVENCHY there and later became his master tailor. Showed first collection in his own house in January 1962. Designed costumes for Rio de Janeiro Carnival in 1965; a men's wear collection in 1970. A superb tailor, noted especially for his coats, he continues in the late 1970s to produce beautifully cut clothes, very elegant and easy.

Versace, Gianni

(Italian ready-to-wear designer)

1978

Well known in the United States. Does four collections—Gianni Versace and Callaghan are the most innovative, Genny and Complice more commercial.

Clothes are expensive, exquisitely made in beautiful fabrics, shown with great professionalism and imaginative accessories. In the United States they have received the status accolade of separate in-store boutiques.

3

AMERICAN DESIGNERS

Adolfo
Adri
Aimbez, Gil
Anthony, John
Assatly, Richard
Atkinson, Bill
Avellino, Dominick
Barrie, Scott
Beene, Geoffrey
Blass, Bill
Brooks, Donald
Burrows, Stephen
Capraro, Albert
Cashin, Bonnie
Cassini, Oleg
Cesarani, Sal
Cipullo, Aldo
Claiborne, Liz
Cummings, Angela
de la Renta, Oscar
Dell'Olio, Louis
Eiseman, Florence
Ellis, Perry
Estevez, Luis
Fuller, Jack
Galanos, James
Gernreich, Rudi
Gerrard, Mady
González, Betsy
Haire, Bill
Halston
Hardwick, Cathy
Harp, Holly
Herman, Stan
Horn, Carol
Johnson, Betsey
Kahn, Robin
Kaiserman, Bill
Kamali, Norma
Karan, Donna
Kasper, Herbert
Kieselstein-Cord, Barry
Kirk, Alexis

Kleibacker, Charles
Klein, Calvin
Kline, Don
Kloss, John
Lane, Kenneth Jay
Latimer, Hubert
Lauren, Ralph
Leal, Ron
Maxwell, Vera
McFadden, Mary
Muto, Anthony
Narducci, Leo
Olive, Frank
Parnis, Mollie
Peretti, Elsa
Rompollo, Dominic
Ruffin, Clovis
Sachs, Gloria
Sanchez, Fernando
Sant'Angelo, Giorgio
Scaasi, Arnold
Schlumberger, Jean
Selwyn, Harriet
Shields, Alexander
Sibley, Joan
Simpson, Adele
Smith, Willi
Stavropoulos, George
Suppon, Charles
Sylbert, Viola
Tassell, Gustave
Tice, Bill
Tiffeau, Jacques
Tilley, Monika
Trigère, Pauline
Van der Akker, Koos
Vass, Joan
Von Furstenberg, Diane
Wacs, Ilie
Weinberg, Chester
Weitz, John
Winter, Harriet
Woods, Wayne

Adolfo (Adolfo Sardina)

(American designer)

BORN: Havana, Cuba, 1929.

AWARDS:
   1955, 1969—Coty American
   Fashion Critics' Special
   Award

1977

1975

Early interest in fashion fostered by aunt, Maria Lopez, a perennial on international "best-dressed" lists, who took him to Paris to see designer showings, introduced him to BALENCIAGA and CHANEL. He began career as an apprentice to Balenciaga. Came to New York in 1948 as millinery designer for Bragaard; went to Emme in 1953; became known as Adolfo of Emme in 1956.

In 1962, Adolfo opened his own millinery firm, gradually added wrap skirts, capes, sleeveless shifts, finally shifting completely into apparel. He has gained and held a loyal clientele for the way he understands and meets their fashion needs and through his ability to turn current trends into flattering, wearable clothes, among the top status symbols of the 1970s. He has chosen to keep his company small, selling to private customers from his Madison Avenue salon and wholesale to a handful of top specialty stores.

Among his successes: the Panama planter's hat, 1966; shaggy Cossack hat, 1967; huge fur berets; such non-hats as fur hoods, kidskin bandanas, and long braids entwined with flowers to be attached to one's own hair. "Romantic look" appeared in 1968 with gingham dirndl skirts, lacy white cotton blouses, ribbons, sashes, big floppy straw hats. In homage to Chanel he introduced a series of knits inspired by her famous tweed suits; these proved so popular he has continued to show variations in every collection. He is also known for beautifully tailored coats and suits; extravagant evening clothes in magnificent fabrics and subtle color combinations.

Adolfo perfume appeared in September 1978; his interests also extend to men's wear, active sportswear, accessories.

Small, shy, with blond hair, brown eyes, a gentle manner, Adolfo's main loves are flowers and fashion.

99

Adri (Adrienne Steckling)

(American designer)

BORN: St. Joseph, Missouri.

MEMBER:
Council of Fashion
Designers of America

Studied design at Washington University, St. Louis. In the 1950s, during her sophomore year, was a guest editor for the college issue of *Mademoiselle* magazine. Came to New York to continue studies at Parsons School of Design where CLAIRE McCARDELL was one of her teachers. McCardell, with her belief in functional, comfortable clothes that move with the body, was, and continues to be, an important influence on Adri's design thinking.

After Parsons Adri went to work at B. H. Wragge, stayed for eight years then opened her own small business. Quickly made a name, but little money; went on to have her name on a number of collections, leisure wear as well as ready-to-wear, each serving to further develop her ideas.

She has always made soft clothes in the McCardell manner to counterbalance the frequent harshness and angularity of the modern environment. She prefers to work with pliant fabrics such as jerseys, knits, challis, crêpe de Chine, and leather; believes that styles should evolve naturally from one collection to the next so that a customer can collect them, add to them, mix them freely from season to season.

Invited in October 1971 to show her clothes at the Smithsonian Institution, Washington D.C. The theme of the two-designer showing was Innovative Contemporary Fashion, with the first part a Claire McCardell retrospective.

Adri is tall and rangy, lives in a remodeled loft south of New York City's flower district. Her interests closely parallel those of her ideal customer: she likes to cook, loves travel, enjoys contemporary dance, films, jazz.

Aimbez, Gil

(American designer)

BORN: Los Angeles, California,
19 May 1940.

Studied fashion illustration at Venice High School; won drawing scholarship to Chouinard School of Art. At 17, went to Frank Wiggins Trade School, taking full fashion design curriculum; won Silver Thimble award for evening clothes, Gold Thimble for sportswear.

Worked in Los Angeles as assistant designer, in turn for Bill Pearson, Ted Small, Dominique Jones. Came to New York as replacement salesperson for Jones, then moved to New York after she closed her Los Angeles business. Went with ANNE KLEIN as assistant and pattern maker; continued to work on Seventh Avenue for various designers for more than seven years.

Joined Peter Clements in fall 1973 to design the Genre collections of separates, sportswear, cruise-wear, evening clothes; became a partner. Bon Menage for dresses was added in spring 1977; Snafu for coats, suits, rainwear and outerwear jackets in spring 1978, with Aimbez responsible for designing in all three divisions.

Aimbez aims for innovation in shape, color, and combinations of texture and fabric within a classic frame; purity and simplicity of line are his primary concerns; he designs his own fabrics. His clothes are in the moderate-to-better price range, known for excellent fit, fine detail, a touch of luxury. He has been praised for his youthful outlook and sense of humor, his feeling for color, texture, superb detailing.

Anthony, John (born Gianantonio Iorio)

(American designer)

BORN: New York City, 1938.

AWARDS:
Coty American Fashion Critics' Award:
1972—"Winnie"
1976—Return Award

Attended High School of Industrial Arts (now High School of Art and Design) where he won three scholarships to train in Europe. Studied one year at the Academia d'Arte in Rome; returned to New York City and studied two years at the Fashion Institute of Technology.

At 19 found first job with Devonbrook where he designed junior clothes for nine years, followed by three years with Adolph Zelinka. John Anthony, Inc. formed January 1971 with Robert Levine, aimed at producing high fashion at moderate-to-better prices.

First design successes under his own name were in coats and suits noted for masterly tailoring and refined elegance. Anthony favors slim, willowy shapes and natural fabrics, has been called "the minimalist of American fashion." He prefers to confine himself in each collection to a few lean, simple shapes, a limited

1977

color palette, a few key textures such as knits, chiffon, cashmere, and charmeuse. His clothes in the late 1970s are young, sophisticated and feminine, marked by unconstructed tailoring, a feeling for asymmetry, ruffles, a sensuous suppleness.

The Anthony name has now been added to men's clothing, shirts, neckwear, sweaters and rainwear; he has designed men's and women's furs for Jan Originals.

Anthony lives in Manhattan, collects Chinese screens and porcelains, is an enthusiastic skier. He travels frequently to Europe in search of fabrics.

1979

Assatly, Richard

(American designer)

BORN: Brooklyn, New York, 8 April 1944.

Father was in the loungewear business. After moving to New Jersey, Richard attended Princeton High School, then studied business administration at Ryder College. Graduated from Fashion Institute of Technology in 1965. Assistant to Pat Sandler, 1965–1968; designer for Ginala, 1968–1974. In 1975, formed Richard Assatly for Gino Snow in partnership with Gino De Georgio, which in January 1978 became Richard Assatly Ltd.

Assatly designs a complete line in the moderate-to-better price range: dresses, suits, coats, separates, evening clothes, even belts. He is completely in touch with current trends and interprets them for a customer he sees as energetic and intelligent, always on the go, a woman of any age. He feels that color and texture are most influential in his work—"color sets the mood"—is convinced that clothes should be practical yet humorous, should make life more beautiful. In addition to his own firm, he designs for Simplicity Patterns.

He relaxes with gymnastics and swimming; is interested in interior design, music, dance.

Atkinson, Bill

(American designer)

BORN: Troy, New York,
22 February 1916.

AWARDS:
1978—Coty American
Fashion Critics' "Winnie"

Graduated from Cornell University, B.A. degree in landscape design, M.A. degree in architecture. From 1937 to 1945 worked in succession for Metro-Goldwyn-Mayer, Houses Inc., Chrysler Corporation; private architectural practice, 1945 to 1950.

Career in clothes design began by accident during World War II. At that time, government regulations severely restricted the yardage used in clothing with skirts limited to a single yard. Atkinson bought eight cotton bandanas at the dime store and on his drawing table put together a skirt for his first wife to wear to a square dance. Other women at the dance wanted the skirt, thirty skirts led to hundreds, then thousands. Looking around for a contractor to handle the orders, Atkinson joined forces in 1950 with a Mr. Glen who had a housedress factory, an association which lasted twenty years. Their operation became Glen of Michigan specializing in a men's wear look for women.

In 1970 he formed a design consulting firm called Presentation. Bill Atkinson, Ltd. was established in 1973 to produce sportswear-oriented clothes in the designer category, aimed at a sophisticated, urban, active customer in the thirty-to-sixty-year age bracket.

In the late 1970s there are plans for a Bill Atkinson licensing program involving leather goods, shoes, women's accessories, sport furs, home furnishings.

A man of many talents and enormous energy, Atkinson is known for impeccable taste, his mastery of fabric combinations, a sophisticated and subtle use of color. He is an excellent photographer, a graphics designer; designed the interior of his showroom, redesigned his country place and planned its garden. For recreation, he prefers gardening and swimming.

Avellino, Dominick

(American designer)

BORN: New York City,
20 January 1944.

Studied art and design; wanted to be a painter; worked in display, flower arranging, interior design. Involved in 1968 with health food-crafts-plant-hippie movement in town near Woodstock, New York; learned to knit and crochet; took up jewelry design.

Moved back to New York in 1969 and with partner

Jeffrey Schwager opened a shop to sell jewelry and knits made by himself and friends. Called it "DDDominick" from the way he stuttered his name as a child.

In 1970 the pair joined Huk-A-Poo, a junior sweater firm. Avellino spent two years commuting to Hong Kong, working out knit patterns, shapes, yarns. He and Schwager left to open own showroom for knits; joined Benson and Partners in 1973; in 1975 left to form DDDominick Sportswear, a young, sophisticated collection in misses sizes at slightly above moderate prices. The Dominick Avellino designer collection was established in 1978.

Avellino thinks of his customer as an active young woman, knowledgeable about fashion, who thinks in terms of a total style. For her he designs sportswear and dresses, suits and coats.

Since 1975, has designed for the McCall Pattern Company under the DDDominick label.

Barrie, Scott

(American designer)

1973

One of several black designers who came to prominence in the 1960s. Raised in Philadelphia; his godmother was a dressmaker, influencing his interest in fashion. Studied applied art for two years at Philadelphia Museum College of Art; attended Mayer School of Fashion in New York.

First design job was for the Allen Cole boutique in 1966; formed partnership in 1969 with Robbie Wolfe, a former model; in late 1970s firm has several divisions.

From the beginning, Barrie has excelled with matte jersey and chiffon evening dresses and pajamas, often with asymmetrical draping, sexy yet refined and elegant.

In addition to ready-to-wear, projects include jewelry, hats, scarves, furs, men's wear. He designed costumes for the Joffrey Ballet's 1973 production of *Deuce Coupe;* has also done film work.

Beene, Geoffrey

(American designer)

BORN: Haynesville, Louisiana, 30 August 1927.

AWARDS:
  Coty American Fashion
    Critics' Award:
    1964—"Winnie"
    1966—Return Award
    1974—Hall of Fame
    1977—Hall of Fame
    Citation (for leadership in
    promoting respect for
    American fashion abroad)
  1964–1965—Neiman-Marcus
    Award

Took pre-med and medicine three years at Tulane University, New Orleans; gave it up, was sent to Southern California by his family. Worked briefly in display at I. Magnin, Los Angeles, where his talent was recognized by an executive who suggested he make fashion a career. Moved to New York to attend Traphagen School of Fashion; went to Paris to study sketching, designing, sewing, at Académie Julian; while in Paris worked for MOLYNEUX, master of tailoring and of the bias cut. Returned to New York in 1949; designer for Samuel Winston, 1949 to 1950; Harmay, 1950 to

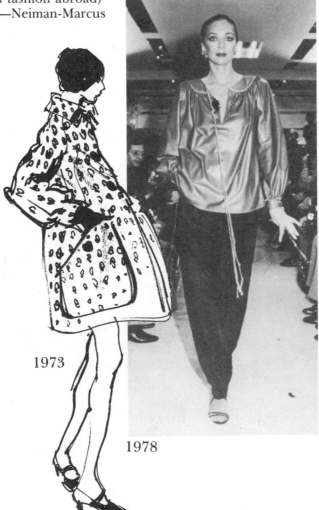

1973

1978

1969

1957; Teal Traina, who put Beene name on the label, 1958 to 1962. Left in 1962 to open business under his own name.

First collection shown in spring 1963 had characteristics of his work throughout the 1960s: looser fit, eased waistlines, bloused tops, flared skirts. He endeavored to achieve greater simplicity in each succeeding collection, increasing emphasis on cut and line, enlivened by special attention to dressmaking details and unusual fabrics. Each showing always included at least one style designed with tongue in cheek to stir things up—a black coat made of wood buttons, a "tutu" evening dress with sequined bodice and feather skirt. In the late 1960s he branched out into furs, swimwear, jewelry, scarves. Designed wedding dress for Lynda Bird Johnson, 1968; first men's wear collection, 1969; started boutique collection, "Beene Bag," 1970.

In 1975 Beene accepted an invitation to show his clothes in Milan, with such success that he decided to manufacture and distribute in Europe. Beene Bag now being made in Canada and Japan. Licenses extend to shoes, gloves, hosiery, eyeglasses, loungewear, sheets, towels, comforters, furniture, and more. Has two fragrances for women and one for men.

Some memorable Beene designs: long, sequined evening gowns cut like oversized football jerseys, complete with numerals; tweed evening pants paired with jeweled or lamé jackets; long-sleeved, grey "sweatshirt" bathing suit.

He is noted for his subtle and imaginative use of color, accenting neutrals with dashes of pure intensities. With him the design stems from the qualities of the fabric and he enjoys mixing "poor" and "rich" materials to achieve a modern look. His design philosophy is that clothes must not only look attractive but must move well, be comfortable to wear, easy to pack; hemlines and lengths are unimportant.

Beene has a fondness for good food. He likes to entertain friends at dinners at home; collects regional cookbooks, paintings, antiques, stamps; finds gardening most rewarding.

Blass, Bill

(American designer)

BORN: Fort Wayne, Indiana, 22 June 1922.

AWARDS:
Coty American Fashion Critics Award:
1961—"Winnie"
1963—Return Award
1968—First Coty Award for Men's Fashion Design
1970—Hall of Fame
1971—Hall of Fame Citation (for overall excellence)
1975—Special Award for Fur design (for Revillon America)
1969—Neiman-Marcus Award
MEMBER:
Council of Fashion Designers of America (former vice president)

Graduated Fort Wayne High School, 1938. Began in fashion in 1940 as sketch artist for David Crystal; served in army in World War II; returned to work as designer for Anna Miller & Co. in 1946 and continued in same capacity when that company merged with Maurice Rentner. Became vice president at Rentner in 1961; formed Bill Blass, Ltd. in 1970, president and principal owner.

Blass is a leading member of the New York couture, in the sense of luxury ready-to-wear. He produces high-priced, high-quality investment clothes, beautifully made from exquisite materials. His customer has an active social life and he is admired for his glamorous, feminine evening clothes, often with an abundance of lace, ruffles or feathers. His daytime fashions are elegant and simple, notable for the refined cut, the excellence of the tailoring, for interesting mixtures of patterns in knits, tweeds, shirtings, expertly coordinated for a polished, worldly look.

1979

In addition to his clothes for women his design projects include: rainwear, 1965; men's clothing and Vogue patterns, 1968; women's sportswear and scarves, 1970; loungewear, 1975; a women's perfume, 1978. In 1974 he designed an automobile, also uniforms for American Airlines' flight attendants.

Brooks, Donald

(American designer)

BORN: New York City, 10 January 1928.

AWARDS:
1962—National Cotton Award
Coty American Fashion Critics' Award:
1958—Special Award
1962—"Winnie"
1967—Return Award
1963—New York Drama Critics Award for costumes (for No Strings)
1974—Parsons Medal for Distinguished Achievement

Studied at Fine Arts School of Syracuse University, 1947 to 1949; Parsons School of Design, New York City, 1949 and 1950. Founded Donald Brooks, Inc., 1965; boutique in 1969. Since 1973 has freelanced, including better dresses and a full collection for Albert Nipon.

Brooks is noted for uncluttered day clothes in clear, unusual colors; careful detailing; dramatic prints of his own design; romantic evening clothes.

Has designed extensively for theater and film. Stage and screen credits include costumes for Diahann Carroll in the Broadway musical, No Strings; for Liza Minelli in the movie, Flora the Red Menace; for Julie Andrews in the movies Star and Darling Lili. He has also designed furs, bathing suits, men's wear, shoes, costume jewelry, wigs, bed linens.

Burrows, Stephen

(American designer)

BORN: Newark, New Jersey.

AWARDS:
Coty American Fashion Critics' Award:
1974—Special Award (lingerie)
1977—"Winnie"

Always loved clothes, started making them as a young boy under the direction of his grandmother. Studied at Philadelphia Museum College of Art and Fashion Institute of Technology in New York.

Joined forces in 1968 with Roz Rubenstein, an F.I.T. classmate, to open boutique; in 1969 both went to work for Henri Bendel—Rubenstein as accessory buyer, Burrows as designer in residence. In 1973 they formed a partnership and opened a firm on Seventh Avenue. Returned to Bendel's in 1977, to work with Pat Tennant.

From the beginning Burrows has been in the advance of fashion, known for his young, flirty cut, and unique color combinations. In the early 1960s he used patches of color for a mosaic effect in dresses and separate tops. Instead of hemming skirts he stitched the edges so they wouldn't ravel, resulting in a fluted effect that became known as "lettuce" hems; top-stitched seams in contrasting colors. He works in soft, clinging fabrics such as chiffon and matte jersey, is addicted to the asymmetrical ". . . there's something nice about something wrong," is the way he puts it.

In addition to ready-to-wear, Burrows designs sleepwear and loungewear, furs, McCall's patterns; in 1978 added hats, costume jewelry. In November 1973, he was one of five American designers to show collections in France at the benefit for the Versailles Palace.

Stephen Burrows and models, 1979

Capraro, Albert

(American designer)

BORN: New York City,
20 May 1943.

AWARDS:
1975–1976—Salvation Army
Auxiliary (outstanding
American designer award
for the Bicentennial)
1975—Fashion Sales Guild,
New York

Attributed his interest in clothes to his grand-mother, who instilled in him a respect for their beauty and for the way they were made. Graduated Parsons School of Design. Worked as associate to LILLY DACHÉ in 1964; associate designer to OSCAR DE LA RENTA from 1966 to 1974; joined forces with Ben Shaw and Jerry Guttenberg in 1974.

Capraro is dedicated to "romantic and feminine clothes combining luxury, ease and comfort." He likes easy shapes in fresh, clear, young colors. First public notice came when Mrs. Gerald Ford, then First Lady, saw a story and photographs of his designs in a Washington newspaper and invited him to bring his collection to the White House.

For recreation he turns to swimming, riding, gardening; loves to travel.

Cashin, Bonnie

(American designer)

BORN: Oakland, California,
1915.

AWARDS:
1950—Neiman-Marcus
Award
Coty American Fashion
Critics' Award:
1950—"Winnie"
1961—Special Award
(leather and fabric design)
1968—Return Award
1972—Hall of Fame

Third generation Californian, raised in San Francisco; mother was a custom dressmaker. Studied at Art Students League of New York. Early career involved with theater, ballet, motion pictures. Among her sixty picture credits were *Anna and the King of Siam* and *Laura.* Moved to New York in 1949, did collections for sportswear houses Adler and Adler and Philip Sills. Free lance after 1952.

Cashin is considered one of the most innovative of American designers, working in her own idiom, uninfluenced by Paris. She believes in functional layers of clothing and showed this way of dressing long before it became an international fashion. From the beginning, she specialized in comfortable clothes for country and travel, using wool jersey, knits, canvas, leather, tweeds in subtle, misty colors. Signature details have been leather bindings, toggles and similar hardware for closings; she has always coordinated her clothes with hoods, bags, boots, belts, of her own design. Like many designers she finds ideas in travel and in ethnic

1973

costumes; Japan, India, Portugal, Italy have been her itinerary.

Among the dominant Cashin themes: the toga cape, the kimono coat, the shell coat, a sleeveless leather jerkin, the poncho, the bubble top, the hooded jersey dress, the long, fringed, mohair plaid at-home skirt.

Cassini, Oleg

(Fashion and costume designer)

BORN: Paris, France, 11 April 1913.

Spent youth in Florence where mother ran a dressmaking salon; graduate of Academia Belle Arti, Florence. Began his fashion career sketching for PATOU. At age 20 established his own couture salon in Rome; came to New York in 1936; worked as designer on Seventh Avenue; opened salon on Madison Avenue in 1937. In 1939 went to Hollywood to design for Paramount Pictures; moved to 20th Century Fox in 1942.

In 1950, returned to New York, formed Oleg Cassini, Inc. for women's apparel. Retired in middle 1960s; set up ready-to-wear business in Milan in partnership with brother Igor. In the late 1970s his name appears on a men's wear collection sold internationally, and also on various paper wares and accessories.

Cassini is best known as official couturier to Jacqueline Kennedy Onassis, a personal friend, during her White House years, and for sexy, fitted dresses with daring decolletages. He claims to have been first, in 1950, with the fitted sheath and with the use of knits.

Cesarani, Sal (S.J.)

(American designer for men and women)

BORN: New York City, 25 September 1939.

AWARDS:
Coty American Fashion Critics' Award:
1974—Special Men's Wear Award
1976—Men's Wear Award

Son of Italian immigrants working in garment industry. Attended High School of Fashion Industries; graduated Fashion Institute of Technology, 1967.

Junior designer at Bobbie Brooks, 1967 to 1969; men's wear coordinator at Paul Stuart, 1969 to 1971; at Polo Fashions, assistant to Ralph Lauren for men's and women's fashions, 1971 to 1973; Country Britches, 1973 to 1975; Stanley Blacker, 1975 to 1976; formed Cesarani Ltd. in 1976, added women's apparel in 1977.

Cesarani is essentially a traditionalist, handling modern trends in a classic way and aiming for quality at a reasonable price. He prefers natural fibers or the look of them, especially British woolens and Harris tweeds for fall, linens for spring and summer.

In late 1970s served as critic at Parsons School of Design; taught men's wear at F.I.T. Recreational preferences are tennis, swimming, dancing, bicycling.

Cipullo, Aldo

(American jewelry designer)

BORN: Rome, Italy, 18 November 1936.

AWARDS:
1974—Coty American Fashion Critics' Special Men's Wear Award (jewelry)
1977—Diamonds Today Competition

Family owned large costume jewelry firm in Italy; Cipullo studied at University of Rome; came to New York in 1959; attended School of Visual Arts.

Worked as designer at David Webb, Tiffany, Cartier. Opened own design studio in 1974.

At Cartier, Cipullo designed the gold "love bracelet" for men and women that fastened with a screw, came with its own small vermeil screwdriver. He has enlarged the scope of men's jewelry with bracelets such as the wrap-around gold nail; lapel pins to replace the boutonniere for evening; as well as pendants, rings, cuff links, studs, buttons.

His design projects extend from jewelry to silverware to textiles, place mats, china, stationery, leather goods, desk accessories. His design objectives are simplicity, elegance, function and style.

For relaxation, he chooses swimming, meditation, cooking.

Claiborne, Liz

(American designer)

BORN: Brussels, Belgium.

Daughter of banker; early childhood spent in New Orleans. Studied painting in Belgium and France. In 1949 won *Harper's Bazaar* national design contest, the prize a trip to Europe; turned to fashion design. On return to United States, Claiborne became a model sketcher, then an assistant to Tina Leser for two years; worked as assistant to Omar Khayam and others; became top designer at Youth Guild, staying sixteen years. Formed Liz Claiborne, Inc. in February 1976 with husband Arthur Ortenberg as business manager.

Claiborne's strength lies in transforming new trends into understandable and salable sportswear. She is known for a sensitive use of color influenced by her fine arts background; for an excellent technical knowledge of fabric and color; for simple, supple, uncomplicated lines. She strives for an easy, natural effect with drama achieved through color and line. Her clothes are in the moderate price range.

She has served as critic for the Fashion Institute of Technology, is the recipient of numerous awards from retailers and industry associations.

Cummings, Angela

(Jewelry designer)

Daughter of German diplomat. Graduate of Zeichenakademie in Hanau, West Germany; studied at Art Academy of Perugia, Italy. Joined Tiffany & Co., 1967. Married in 1970 to Bruce Cummings, gemmologist and Tiffany vice president.

Cummings is thoroughly versed in gemmology and goldsmithing as well as in jewelry design. Her work is in the classic vein but far from traditional, often combining materials such as wood, gold and diamonds. She has also revived old techniques such as damascene, the ancient art of inlaying iron with precious metal. Much of her inspiration comes from nature; for example, silver jewelry derived from the leaf of a gingko tree.

She and her husband live in Connecticut where she indulges a passion for gardening. They share space with their Abyssinian cats, some semi-tame raccoons, a wild Canada goose.

de la Renta, Oscar

(American designer)

BORN: Santo Domingo, Dominican Republic, 22 July 1932.

AWARDS:
Coty American Fashion Critics' Award:
  1967—"Winnie"
  1968—Return Award
  1973—Hall of Fame
1968—Neiman-Marcus Award
Numerous awards from the Dominican Republic

Educated in Santo Domingo and Madrid; remained in Madrid after graduation to study art, intending to become a painter. Fashion career began when sketches made for fun were seen by the wife of the American ambassador to Spain, who asked him to design gown for her daughter's debut.

First professional job was with BALENCIAGA's Madrid couture house, "Eisa"; went to Paris in 1961 as assistant to Antonio de Castillo at Lanvin-Castillo; to New York in 1963 with Castillo to design at Elizabeth Arden. Joined Jane Derby in 1965; soon was operating as Oscar de la Renta, Ltd. producing luxury ready-to-wear.

De la Renta is known for romantic evening clothes in opulent materials and for the imaginative use of transparent fabrics; his day clothes have gained importance in the late 1970s.

Added a boutique line in 1966; men's wear in 1968; "Something by Oscar de la Renta" in 1971; perfume in 1977. Has also done bathing suits, wedding dresses, furs, jewelry, bed linens.

Married to Françoise de Langlade, former editor of French *Vogue,* in 1967. He is active in the Rehabilitation Center for Mentally Retarded Children in Santo Domingo.

1979

Dell'Olio, Louis

(American designer)

BORN: New York City,
23 July 1948.

AWARDS:
1977—Coty American
Fashion Critics' "Winnie"
(with Donna Karan for
Anne Klein & Co.)

Received Norman Norell Scholarship to Parsons School of Design, 1967; graduated Parsons, 1969; won Gold Thimble Award for coats and suits.

Assistant to DOMINIC ROMPOLLO at Teal Traina, 1969 to 1971; designer at Giorgini and Ginori divisions of Originala, 1971 to 1974; since 1974 co-designer with DONNA KARAN at Anne Klein & Co., Inc.

Dell'Olio and Karan have brought a very modern, totally sophisticated interpretation to the classic ANNE KLEIN sportswear. They work with easy shapes in beautiful fabrics; the clothes are in the deluxe investment category. Their design projects include furs for Michael Forrest.

For relaxation, Dell'Olio likes to paint, enjoys swimming.

Eiseman, Florence

(American designer of children's clothes)

BORN: Minneapolis, Minnesota,
27 September 1899.

AWARDS:
1955—Neiman-Marcus
Award (the first children's
designer to receive it)

Married to Laurence H. Eiseman, 1927; two sons. Since 1945, successively vice-president, president, chairman, of Florence Eiseman, Inc.

After sons went off to college in 1940s, started making organdy pinafores for children of friends; husband took samples to Marshall Field & Co., obtaining a $3,000 first order which sold out in a month. This enabled her to set up a business consisting of one seamstress and one sewing machine, Mrs. Eiseman as designer, her husband as business manager-salesman. Within a few years the Milwaukee-based firm grew into a large business, making clothes sold across the United States and abroad.

In an era of fussy children's clothes, Eiseman produced simple styles distinguished by fine fabrics and excellent workmanship, with prices to match. She became known as the NORMAN NORELL of children's clothes, making dresses, jumpers, skirts, blouses, boys' suits, swimsuits, beach jackets, play clothes, and sleepwear. In 1969 she added knits, as well as mother-daughter and brother-sister outfits.

Ellis, Perry

(American designer)

BORN: Virginia, 1940.

AWARDS:
  1979—Neiman-Marcus
    Award
  1979—Coty American
    Fashion Critics' "Winnie"

Grew up in Portsmouth, Virginia; attended William and Mary College; took M.A. degree in retailing from New York University. Worked in Richmond as sportswear buyer for Miller & Rhoads; spent six years with John Meyer of Norwich, a conservative sportswear firm, working on color and fabric choices; joined the Vera companies in 1974 as vice president in charge of merchandising a sportswear line; in 1976 became designer for Portfolio, a division of Vera. In 1978, Manhattan Industries, which owns Vera, established a new division, Perry Ellis, with Ellis as president and designer.

Ellis prefers natural fibers—cottons, silks, linens, woolens—mostly in natural colors. He shows sweaters knitted of unbleached, undyed sheep's wool, silks that look like tweeds, tweeds in subtle color mixtures, everything tending to look hand-loomed. The clothes are individualistic, with a free, young spirit; are made of good fabrics and retail at moderate prices. They reflect his philosophy that people should not be too concerned with what they wear.

He divides his private life between his West Side brownstone and a house on Fire Island; dislikes big parties; likes to read, cook, exercise, dance; loves film.

1979

Estevez, Luis

(American designer)

BORN: Havana, Cuba, 1932.

AWARDS:
1956—Coty American Fashion Critics' "Winnie"

MEMBER:
Council of Fashion Designers of America (charter member)

Son of sugar magnate. Attended prep school in United States; returned to Havana to study architecture; took summer job in display department of Lord & Taylor, New York City, never returned to architecture. Studied cutting and draping at the Traphagen School of Fashion; worked with a Seventh Avenue dress firm; went to Paris and spent one and a half years at PATOU before returning to New York. Has lived and worked in California since 1968; designed for Eva Gabor International in 1972; headed own division of Beneficial Corporation, 1974 to 1977; since 1977 heads his own firm.

Estevez aims for restrained elegance in reasonably priced fabrics for the mass market. He is known for sexy cocktail and evening dresses with unusual cut-out necklines; a frequent use of black-and-white; dramatic accessories. Has also designed furs, swimwear, men's wear, for firms on both coasts.

Fuller, Jack

(American designer)

BORN: Visalia, Georgia, 30 December 1945.

AWARDS:
Since 1973 has received recognition from such diverse sources as The Hecht Co., the University of Cincinnati, Joseph Schlitz Brewing Co.

Graduated J.D. Dickerson High School, 1962; Parsons School of Design in New York, 1965.

Worked on Seventh Avenue at KASPER for Joan Leslie, 1968 to 1970; Elliott Boss, 1970 to 1972; 1973 to 1975 with a number of firms including one stint in furs. Beginning in 1976 designed separates and dresses, retailing from $40 to $140, at Jardine Ltd.; showed first collection as Jack Fuller Ltd., 1978.

His aim is to produce sophisticated clothes as sensible prices.

Fuller also makes needlepoint designs.

For recreation he likes theater, travel, entertaining; enjoys baseball and football.

Galanos, James

(American designer)

BORN: Philadelphia,
Pennsylvania, 20 September
1925.

AWARDS:
1954—Neiman-Marcus
Award
Coty American Fashion
Critics' Award:
1954—"Winnie"
1956—Return Award
1959—Hall of Fame

EXHIBITION:
1976—"Galanos—25 Years"
—Special fashion show
and exhibition at Fashion
Institute of Technology
celebrating his twenty-fifth
year in business

Son of Greek parents. Entered fashion design school in New York, after a few months began selling sketches to manufacturers. Worked with HATTIE CARNEGIE in 1944; went to Paris where he worked with ROBERT PIGUET, 1947–1948; returned to New York and designed for Davidow. Went to Los Angeles where he did film work with Jean Louis, who helped him start his own business in 1951. First New York showing in 1953 in a private apartment launched him on a spectacular career.

Widely considered the greatest, most independent designer working in America today and the equal of the great Paris couturiers, Galanos produces ready-to-wear that has become a symbol of luxury at prices

1963

1962

comparable to couture. He is known for the purity of his line, for intricate construction and flawless workmanship in magnificent imported fabrics. His designs over the years show consistency of viewpoint from the shifts of the early years to tailored suits to bouffant evening dresses; his beautiful chiffons are especially famous. An exacting perfectionist, he designs the complete look for his showings: hairdos, shoes, makeup, hats, hosiery, accessories.

Because he likes the climate and relaxed living style, he lives and works in California, where he has assembled a workroom of near-miraculous proficiency and skill.

Gernreich, Rudi

(American designer)

BORN: Vienna, Austria, 8 August 1922.

AWARDS:
Coty American Fashion
Critics' Award:
1963—"Winnie"
1966—Return Award
1967—Hall of Fame
1975—Crystal Ball Award of the Knitted Textile Association

As a boy, thought of becoming a painter; had early exposure to fashion and learned about fabrics and dressmaking while sketching in his aunt's couture salon. With his mother, left Austria for California, 1938; became United States citizen, 1943. Attended

Rudi Gernreich and model, 1968

Los Angeles City College, 1938 to 1941; Los Angeles Art Center School, 1941 to 1942.

Spent five years as a dancer with Lester Horton Dance Theatre before turning to fashion as a fabric salesperson. Designed a series of dresses to demonstrate fabrics, which aroused so much interest that in 1951 he formed design associations with two California firms.

Considered one of the most original and prophetic designers in the United States. Gernreich's specialties in the 1950s and 1960s were dramatic sport clothes in striking cuts and color combinations. In the 1950s, an age of constructed bathing suits, he created the maillot without an inner bra, bare suits with deeply cut-out sides, and in 1964, the topless bathing suit. He designed the soft "no-bra" bra in skin-toned nylon net; clinging knit minidresses; "Swiss cheese" swim suits; see-through blouses; knee-high leggings patterned to match tunic tops and tights. Took a sabbatical in 1969, 1970, returned with predictions for the future of bald heads, bare bosoms with pasties, unisex caftans. He continues to design on a free-lance basis: knitwear, hosiery, scarves, lingerie, professional dance and exercise clothes; has done a home furnishings group for Knoll International.

Gerrard, Mady

(American designer specializing in knits and crocheted clothes)

BORN: Budapest, Hungary, 27 April 1930.

Educated in Budapest and London. At the age of 5, learned to knit from a great aunt; bought first knitting machine in Cardiff, South Wales, where she also opened her first boutique. Later had boutiques in London and Toronto, Canada, before arriving in New York in 1969.

Gerrard concentrates on luxurious daytime and evening clothes and accessories in the higher price range; hand-finished knits and crochets in soft yarns—cashmere, mohair, wool—dyed to produce unusual ombréd effects. The clothes are both sophisticated and practical, can be built into a wardrobe by adding pieces.

For recreation she likes to visit museums, loves theater and opera; enjoys travel.

González, Betsy

(American designer)

BORN: Puerto Rico,
    28 December 1950.

In New York, attended Cathedral High, winning honors in fine art; graduated Parsons School of Design, winner of both Chester Weinberg and Donald Brooks awards. In 1976, formed Sonata with associate Alda Abbracciamento.

González designs separates and dresses in luxurious fabrics, as well as coats to wear over them. She works with supple, simplified shapes, her strength, a subtle and harmonious blending of textures and colors. She feels her customer is a woman who likes options, does not want to be dictated to, does want her imagination to be stimulated.

Sketching, painting, writing, are favorite recreations.

Haire, Bill

(American designer)

BORN: New York City.

Attended High School of Industrial Art (now High School of Art and Design); won scholarship to the Fashion Institute of Technology, graduating in 1955. Married in 1956 to Hazel Keleher. Taught evenings at F.I.T. Traveled extensively in Europe in 1958; returned to United States in 1959 and went to work as a designer for Victoria Royal, an evening wear firm. After fourteen years, joined Henry Friedricks & Co. in 1953, a move which allowed him to do a complete range of clothes—sportswear to coats—at first as co-designer with his wife. When she left to design on a free-lance basis, he continued under Bill Haire for Friedricks Sport label.

Haire regards his customer as his equal in design understanding, never underestimates her sophistication; he endeavors to anticipate the direction she is taking in order to give her clothes that meet her changing needs. He prefers to work in natural fibers, tailors them expertly to simple, classic lines, avoiding faddishness, striving for a blend of style and practicality. In the late 1970s he broadened his range to include dresses and suits of a suavity not usually associated with sportswear.

His New York apartment, once filled with antiques collected in thirty-five trips to Europe, has been renovated into a dramatic minimal space. He continues his love for ballet and music.

Halston (Roy Halston Frowick)

(American designer)

BORN: Des Moines, Iowa, 1932.

AWARDS:
Coty American Fashion Critics' Award:
1962, 1969—Special Award
1971—"Winnie"
1972—Return Award
1974—Hall of Fame

Grew up in Evansville, Indiana; attended Indiana University and Chicago Art Institute; designed and sold hats while still a student. Moved to New York in 1957; worked for LILLY DACHÉ; in 1959 joined Berg-

1973

1978

Halston, 1975

dorf Goodman where he gained a name and a fashionable clientele; in the late 1960s started designing ready-to-wear.

In 1968 Halston established his own firm for private clients; Halston International was formed in 1970 for knitwear and accessories; ready-to-wear followed in 1972 with the opening of Halston Originals. Business was acquired by Norton Simon in 1973.

From his early days at Bergdorf's, Halston's influence was felt in the fashion world. He originated the scarf hat, the pillbox hat that Jacqueline Kennedy wore for her husband's inaugural. In the 1970s his formula of using superior fabrics for extremely simple, classic shapes has made him one of the top status designers. Typical are the long cashmere dress with a sweater tied over the shoulders; wrap skirts and turtlenecks; evening caftans; long, slinky, haltered jerseys. He pioneered in the use of Ultra-Suede®; shows his clothes with accessories and jewelry designed by ELSA PERETTI, who also designed the containers for his cosmetics. Name now extends to bodywear, beachwear, luggage, perfume, cosmetics, loungewear, men's wear, furs, jewelry, eyeglasses, wigs, scarves, etc.

Hardwick, Cathy

(American designer)

BORN: Korea,
    30 December 1933.

Studied voice and piano for ten years; went to Japan to study music and after one year came to United States. Opened a boutique in San Francisco for which she designed most of the merchandise, importing the rest. Designed a line of junior knitwear for Alvin Duskin; closed boutique and worked for Duskin and for a Danish firm, Dranella. Moved to New York in late 1960s; did work for Pranx, Exit, Match II, Warner's Lingerie. Opened own design studio in 1972; established manufacturing firm, Cathy Hardwick & Friends, Ltd.

Hardwick is known for clean-cut, fluid clothes, understated but sensuous; she prefers fine, natural fabrics in muted tones, a flash of color in accessories. Her aim is consistency as well as innovation, continuity and evolution rather than drastic changes; she wants her clothes to be comfortable and useful as well as fashionable. She strives for the best possible quality, feels that fashion is a matter of style and taste rather than price.

In addition to clothes, she designs her own prints and jewelry; in 1976, 1977 designed dinnerware for Mikasa; blouses for Dessiner; sheets and towels for WestPoint-Pepperell and J.C. Penney; uniforms; Simplicity Patterns.

Harp, Holly

(American designer)

BORN: Buffalo, New York, 24 October 1939.

MEMBER:
Council of Fashion Designers of America

Holly Harp and model, 1976

Daughter of a machinery designer; dropped out of Radcliffe in sophomore year and went to Acapulco; designed sandals, then clothes to go with them. Returned to school at North Texas State University to study art and fashion design; moved to Los Angeles.

In 1968, with a loan from her father, opened a boutique on Sunset Strip; in 1972 Henri Bendel established a boutique for her clothes; wholesale line started in 1973; clothes now sold in fine specialty stores around the United States.

Holly Harp first became known for costumy, offbeat evening clothes, popular with entertainment figures and rock stars. She soon switched from feathers and fringe to subtler, sophisticated cuts, often on the bias, usually two-piece and in one size. These were elegantly engineered in matte jersey or chiffon, frequently decorated with hand-painted or airbrushed designs.

While essentially very simple, her clothes are unconventional and also expensive, making her customer a free-thinking woman with money. Harp's design philosophy: "Whenever I'm trying to make an aesthetic decision, I always go in the direction of taking chances."

Other design commitments are to Simplicity Patterns, 1978; bed linens for Fieldcrest, 1979.

For recreation, she likes swimming and water skiing.

Herman, Stan

(American designer)

AWARDS:
Coty American Fashion
Critics' Award:
1965—Joint Special Award
for "Young
Contemporaries" design
1969—"Winnie"
1974—Special Award
(lingerie)

Studied applied arts at University of Cincinnati; in New York, went to work for dress house, Herbert Sondheim, at same time attending classes at Traphagen School of Fashion. Gained experience in various Seventh Avenue firms; took singing and dancing lessons during lunch hour and in 1957 deserted fashion for the stage. In 1959, joined Mr. Mort as designer, eventually becoming designer-owner. In the 1970s established a design studio and in April 1978, a new ready-to-wear firm, Stan Herman, essentially a dress house.

Herman is dedicated to producing innovative yet salable clothes at sensible prices for the woman who views fashion as just one part of her life rather than a dominant factor. In the 1960s he led in putting dresses over pants, wrapped women in the bathrobe dress, used pleats in countless imaginative ways. His shapes are clean-lined; his sleep and lounge collection for Kentelle balances comfort and elegance, is easy, refined, expert.

In addition to dresses, Herman creates sleepwear and loungewear; a line of men's leisure wear; designs for Vogue Patterns; has done girdles, bras, body suits, shirts; uniforms for McDonald's, Avis, TWA and in 1978, for United Airlines.

Herman serves as a critic at Parsons School of Design and Pratt Institute; lectures at the Fashion Institute of Technology and at schools across America. He is Seventh Avenue's representative on Community Board No. 5.

He loves classical music and surrounds himself with it at his Manhattan apartment and his house near Southampton; whenever he can find the time he travels to England and Northern Italy.

Horn, Carol

(American designer)

AWARDS:
1975—Coty American
Fashion Critics' "Winnie"

Studied fine arts at Boston University and at Columbia University. Worked as fashion coordinator in retailing before turning to design. Main designer for Bryant 9 junior sportswear firm; sole designer for Benson and Partners for almost four years; designer-director of Carol Horn division of Malcolm Starr; designed sportswear for Carol Horn's Habitat, dresses for C.H.H. In 1979 signed a licensing agreement with Savannah Retail to do classic sportswear, another with Great Times for maternity clothes; established her own firm to produce a more highly styled designer line under the Carol Horn label.

Horn's trademarks are easy, uncontrived shapes in natural fabrics and muted tones, a contemporary feeling; her aim, clothes that are comfortable and seasonless for a moderate price.

Johnson, Betsey

(American designer)

BORN: Wethersfield, Connecticut, 1942.

AWARDS:
1971—Coty American Fashion Critics' "Winnie"

Attended Pratt Institute for one year; graduated cum laude from Syracuse University, member Phi Beta Kappa. In senior year was guest editor at *Mademoiselle* magazine; sweaters she made for editors were seen by owner of Paraphernalia shops who gave her a job designing. These original, irreverent collections established her at age 22 as a leader of the youth-oriented, anti-Seventh Avenue movement of the 1960s.

1966

In 1969, with two friends, started boutique "Betsey, Bunky and Nini"; has designed for Alley Cat, Michael Milea, Butterick Patterns. In July 1978, formed Betsey Johnson, Inc. to manufacture sportswear, bodywear, dresses.

Johnson is unique, imaginative, uninhibited, designing for spirited nonconformists like herself. Typical ideas are the "Basic Betsey," a clinging T-shirt dress in mini, midi or maxi lengths; a clear vinyl slip-dress complete with kit of paste-on stars, fishes and numbers; the "noise" dress with loose grommets at the hem. She designs her own fabrics and knits and has worked in cotton-and-spandex knits, rayon challis, very heavyweight spandex in vibrant colors turning out very body-conscious clothes ranging from bathing to body suits, tight pants to dance dresses.

Kahn, Robin

(American jewelry designer)

BORN: London, England, 12 January 1947.

Arrived in New York in 1952. Studied at Parsons School of Design, Haystack Mountain School of Crafts. Spent seven years in costume jewelry business with KENNETH JAY LANE, OSCAR DE LA RENTA, PIERRE CARDIN. Took special training with creative goldsmiths and for first time made his creations with his own hands. Formed Robin Kahn, Inc. in April 1978.

Kahn has made his name working in three non-precious metals, brass, copper, bronze, combining them for a look that is strong, bold, clean and precise. He also uses ivory, ebony, turquoise, lapis; adds taffeta in different colors, leather cording. His jewelry, which might be called futuristic Art Deco, is in the moderate-to high-priced category and is sold at fine specialty stores across the United States.

Kaiserman, Bill

(American designer for men and women)

BORN: New York City, 8 September 1942.

Educated University of Miami; Herbert Berghoff Drama School. Although without formal training, was involved in fabrics and color since childhood as his family is in the interior design field; always knew he would be a designer without being sure of what area.

AWARDS:
  Coty American Fashion
    Critics' Award:
    1974—Men's Wear Award
    1975—Men's Wear Return
    Award
    1976—Hall of Fame for
    Men's Wear
    1978—Hall of Fame
    Citation (for his continued
    contribution to the growth
    of American men's
    fashion)
MEMBER:
  Council of Fashion
    Designers of America

Since 1968, designer and president of Rafael Fashions, Ltd.; in August 1978 established Bill Kaiserman Ltd., a licensing firm.

While working part-time in a men's boutique, Kaiserman saw a need for improved styling in men's hats and designed a collection, his first use of the "Rafael" label. He arranged for samples and manufacturing, even made deliveries himself. From that beginning he branched out into leather accessories, clothing, outerwear, casual suits, sportswear. His men's designs now break down into two collections, finely tailored clothing and active sportswear.

Meanwhile he produced a limited group of tailored clothes for women, added sportswear, day dresses, evening clothes.. These are beautifully cut and detailed, made in Italy of luxurious European fabrics. For both men and women, Kaiserman tries to achieve individuality yet avoid trendiness, aiming at "unassuming clothing that is casual, precise . . . using natural fibers and earthy colors." The clothes are in the better price range.

Kamali, Norma

(*American designer*)

BORN: New York
  City,
  27 June 1945.

1976

Graduated Fashion Institute of Technology where she studied fashion illustration. For ten years designer for Kamali Ltd.; in March 1978 established OMO Norma Kamali, a retail boutique and wholesale firm.

Imaginative and adventurous, she sees fashion as an art form; although best known for extreme, avant garde clothes, she is committed to fine fabrics and serious design. Her draped and shirred "parachute" designs, using parachute fabric and the drawstrings, were included in the "Vanity Fair" show at the Costume Institute, Metropolitan Museum of Art, New York, 1978; she did costumes for one segment of the Diana Ross film, *The Wiz*.

For relaxation she enjoys camping and swimming.

Karan, Donna

(American designer)

BORN: Forest Hills, New York, 2 October 1948.

AWARDS:
1977—Coty American Fashion Critics' "Winnie" (with Louis Dell'Olio for Anne Klein & Co.)

Daughter of a fashion model and a haberdasher, Karan was steeped in fashion from childhood; at age 14 lied about her age and got a job selling. Enrolled at Parsons School of Design; after second year took summer job with ANNE KLEIN and stayed on instead of returning to school. After nine months was fired, went to work for another sportswear house. Returned to Klein in 1968, became associate designer in 1971; took over design direction in 1974 at Anne Klein's death; since 1974 co-designer with LOUIS DELL'OLIO.

Karan derives a shape from the fabric, not from a sketch. She believes that things must change and should never be allowed to become boring, but that each change must be a logical development and not simply for the sake of change or to make headlines.

Tall and good looking, she is a natural athlete, rides well, enjoys bicycling; is a good cook and "an avid scrubber."

Kasper, Herbert

(American designer)

BORN: New York City, 12 December 1926.

AWARDS:
Coty American Fashion Critics' Award:
1955—"Winnie"
1970—Return Award
1976—Hall of Fame
MEMBER:
Council of Fashion Designers of America (president, 1977)

Attended DeWitt Clinton High School in the Bronx, New York University. Became interested in fashion while in army, designed costumes for army shows when with occupation forces in Germany. Back in New York, attended Parsons School of Design; went to Paris for two years and through the Chambre Syndicale de la Couture, obtained work at various couture houses and at *Elle* magazine. Returned to United States and designed hats for John-Frederics as well as costumes for Broadway revues.

In 1953 went to work for Penart Fashions; joined Arnold & Fox in 1955. Kasper for Joan Leslie Inc., a division of Leslie Fay, established in 1967; Kasper for J. L. Sport Ltd. in 1970; Kasper for Weatherscope in 1977; vice president of Joan Leslie Inc.

From the beginning Kasper has aimed for a couture look at prices acceptable to many women. He is cognizant of current trends and interprets them for a specific American woman who does not like extremes but to whom dressing with style is a part of life. His three main design commitments cover dresses and costumes for day and evening; a more relaxed, sportswear look; suits, coats, rain and storm coats.

Other design projects include furs, handbags, bed linens for Wamsutta.

Kasper enjoys sports, especially tennis, swimming, skiing.

Kieselstein-Cord, Barry

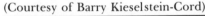

(American jewelry designer)

BORN: New York City.

He comes from several generations of designers and architects in divergent fields, including his mother and father and both grandfathers. Studied in New York at Parsons School of Design, New York University, the American Craft League. Worked in advertising agencies as art director-producer on commercial films. Introduced first jewelry collection in 1972 or 1973 at Georg Jensen; by the late 1970s sold through thirty or more retailers around the United States and exported to other countries. He has made an educational film for the platinum industry; has been creative director of a helicopter support and maintenance company, responsible for all corporate design.

Kieselstein-Cord works mainly in gold and platinum. Each design starts on paper, moves from there

(Courtesy of Barry Kieselstein-Cord)

directly into metal or into wax, depending on whether it will be reproduced by hand or from a mold; each piece is hand-finished before it leaves the studio. He aims at timeless, continuing design values quite separate from fashion saying, "People who wear my jewelry will find it to be an intensely personal statement for a lifetime." His jewelry has been praised for elegance, beauty and superb craftsmanship; has been featured in the fashion and consumer press. Pieces such as the Winchester buckle and palm cuffs are collected by leading fashion designers in the United States and Europe and by celebrities everywhere. Prices are healthy and place his jewelry in the status category.

Both he and his wife love horses and horse competitions; he also enjoys match shooting.

Kirk, Alexis

(American designer)

BORN: Los Angeles, California, 29 December 1938.

AWARDS:
1970—Coty American Fashion Critics' Joint Special Award (costume jewelry)
Several European awards for accessories and jewelry

MEMBER:
Council of Fashion Designers of America
Design America

Attended Cambridge College, Cambridge, Massachusetts, 1955 to 1956; Rhode Island School of Design, 1956 to 1959; studied and taught design and architecture at University of Tennessee, 1959 to 1960; took part in First Congress of Environmental Studies at Harvard, with architect Walter Gropius as chairman, 1960 to 1961.

Established workshop in Newport, Rhode Island, in 1961, then three boutiques called "Derring-Do." Was staff designer at Design Research; for El Greco Fashions, 1968, HATTIE CARNEGIE Inc., 1969. Opened own costume jewelry company in 1970, winning special notice for work in pewter. Currently associated with AVK Designs International with several signature lines; sees "the solution of a problem" as the essence of design, feels he has been strongly influenced by Gropius.

Kirk is interested in all facets of design, is mainly known for jewelry in the middle to upper price range, a preference for natural materials and sculptural lines, combinations of metals and materials, often with exotic results.

His design projects extend to accessories, sportswear, dresses, shoes, handbags, home furnishings, bodywear. Was technical advisor in 1972 and 1975 for costumes, sets and special effects for two films; in 1974 produced and directed film on the history of design for Smithsonian Institution. Contributor to fashion departments of Museum of the City of New York and the Metropolitan Museum of Art.

He is fascinated by fine automobiles, racing cars, bullfighting; loves gourmet food, dance, the theater.

Kleibacker, Charles

(American designer)

BORN: Cullman, Alabama, 20 November 1926.

Majored in journalism at Notre Dame, graduated in 1947; did graduate work in retailing at night at New York University, 1948 to 1950, while working as reporter and as a copywriter at Gimbel's New York under Bernice Fitz-Gibbon. Toured with singer Hildegarde, 1952 to 1955; worked at Lanvin-Castillo, Paris, 1955 to 1958; Nettie Rosenstein, New York, 1958 to 1960; since 1961 has headed own custom design business for special clients and stores.

Kleibacker designs timeless late-day clothes of fluid bias cut, "engineered" to an individual anatomy, soft and lyrical. They are in the deluxe category. He is known for the simplicity and individuality of his cut, for his expert handling of the bias technique, and for exquisite workmanship.

In addition to designing, he lectures extensively on fashion; serves as visiting designer at college fashion design departments including Mount Mary College, Milwaukee, and Virginia Commonwealth University, Richmond; taught at Pratt Institute, New York, 1974 to 1975, 1977; since 1976 consultant to American Silk Mills.

He enjoys swimming and the theater.

Klein, Calvin

(American designer)

BORN: New York City, 1943.

Attended High School of Industrial Art (now High School of Art and Design); graduated from Fashion Institute of Technology, 1962. Spent five years as apprentice and designer at three large firms; in 1968 with Barry Schwartz, a long-time friend, formed Calvin Klein Ltd.

AWARDS:
  Coty American Fashion
    Critics' Award (first
    designer to win awards in
    three consecutive years):
  1973—"Winnie"
  1974—Return Award
  1975—Hall of Fame
  1975—Special Award for
    fur design (for Alixandre)

Klein presents a full wardrobe, day into evening; working in simplified, refined shapes and employing natural fibers such as cashmere, mohair, wool, cotton, silk, as well as leather and suede. He prefers earth tones and neutrals. A modern classicist, he makes clothes with a lean, supple elegance and offhand, understated luxury.

In addition to ready-to-wear, Klein designs furs, umbrellas, scarves, shoes, bags, bed linens. In 1978 introduced cosmetics, skin care and a fragrance, a line of men's wear.

He is a faculty consultant at Parsons School of Design and at Fashion Institute of Technology.

1979

Kline, Don

(American designer)

BORN: Vandergrift (near
Pittsburgh), Pennsylvania.

AWARDS:
1973—Coty American
Fashion Critics' Special
Accessory Award (hats)

Graduated from Fashion Institute of Technology in 1969. Worked for the milliner, Emme, for several years designing hats, clothes, accessories. Designed sportswear for six months; did a series of hats which he took around to fashion magazines and stores, selling enough to open a showroom. In 1976 began making ready-to-wear; opened a retail boutique on Madison Avenue in 1977; in 1978 added furs to his design projects.

Kline is frequently credited with inspiring a revival of interest in hats. Early successes included draped turbans, small tilted felts in the manner of the 1930s and 1940s, an urbane version of the stitched tweed sportsman's hat. For several years he designed hats to complement the collections of other designers. His ready-to-wear, which runs the gamut of day to evening —separates, dresses, "everything"—is marked by the same wit and whimsy as his hats.

Kloss, John (born John Klosowski)

(American designer)

BORN: Detroit, Michigan.

AWARDS:
1971, 1974—Coty American
Fashion Critics' Special
Award (lingerie and
loungewear)

First thought of architecture as a career but switched to finance; in New York at age 18 worked for the Irving Trust Co. and studied fashion at night at Traphagen School of Fashion. Impressed his instructor with his work and was recommended by him to Bob Bugnand in Paris, where Kloss went at age 20 to apprentice. After that he worked briefly with Serge Matta, had an offer from NINA RICCI but decided to return to New York where he co-designed a collection with Lisa Fonssagrives before setting up a custom business of his own.

His soft, free-style clothes in abstract color patterns attracted a clientele of fashionable customers; Gerry Stutz of Henri Bendel liked them so well she established a boutique, the first the store had devoted to a single designer. Kloss was with Bendel's Studio when it first opened, spent a short time on Seventh Avenue then branched out into sleep and loungewear with Cira.

Kloss is best known for clingy, sexy, fluid dresses

with precise, delicate details and for nightgowns and loungewear that are clean-cut in shape, have close-fitting bodices, very deep-cut necklines.

In addition, he designs swimsuits, sportswear, patterns, slippers, needlepoint and sweater kits.

He has so streamlined his schedule that he is able to spend two and a half days in New York, the rest of the time at his one hundred-acre farm in North Blenheim, New York, and more recently, at a home in Florida. He dislikes travel; enjoys working on his farm and tinkering with cars and farm machinery, cooking for friends, collecting antiques.

Lane, Kenneth Jay

(American designer)

BORN: Detroit, Michigan, 22 April 1932.

AWARDS:
  1966—Coty American Fashion Critics' Special Award (jewelry)
  1968—Neiman-Marcus Award

Attended University of Michigan, 1950–1952; graduated from Rhode Island School of Design with B.F.A. degree in 1954. First worked in New York on promotion art staff of *Vogue* magazine and while there met Roger Vivier. Through him, Lane became assistant designer for Delman Shoes, a division of Genesco, then associate designer of Christian Dior Shoes. This allowed him to spend part of each year in Paris working with Vivier.

In 1963, while still designing shoes, Lane made a few pieces of jewelry, primarily earrings. These were photographed by the fashion magazines and bought by a few stores. He continued with shoes, making jewelry at night and on weekends, using his initials K.J.L. for his jewelry. By June 1974 he was able to make jewelry design a full-time career. Kenneth Jay Lane, Inc. became a part of Kenton Corporation in 1969; since 1972 it has been independently owned. Also designs special accessories for the home, decorative and functional.

Like a designer of precious jewelry, Lane first makes his designs in wax or by carving or twisting metal. "I want to make real jewelry with not-real materials." He sees plastic as the modern medium, perfect for simulating real gems, lightweight, available in every color. He likes to see his jewelry intermixed with the real gems worn by his international roster of celebrity customers.

atimer, Hubert

(American designer)

BORN: Atlanta, Georgia,
17 September 1927.

AWARDS:
1973—Maison Blanche
"Rex" Award, New
Orleans

Always wanted to design and sketched dresses for his sister which his mother made. Enrolled at Wolf School of Design in Los Angeles when his family moved to California. In Los Angeles, spent four and a half years as partner in Benjamin-Hubert; designed the Cooper Couture collection for Charles Cooper; worked for Irene of California. In 1970, was signed to design the CHRISTIAN DIOR-New York Collections; joined MOLLIE PARNIS Couture in 1973. In June 1977 established his own firm, Hubert Latimer, Inc. Rejoined MOLLIE PARNIS in 1979 on death of designer Morty Sussman.

Latimer designs for a secure, worldly woman with a definite point of view, someone who will put her own stamp on whatever she wears. He avoids trendiness, works for purity of line, includes at least one forward-looking idea in each collection.

He lives in Manhattan, spends weekends in East Hampton. Interests include gardening, taking photographs, painting, cooking, entertaining four to six people.

Lauren, Ralph

(American designer)

BORN: New York City,
14 October 1939.

AWARDS:
Coty American Fashion
Critics' Award:
1970—Men's Wear Award
1973—Return Men's Wear
Award
1974—"Winnie"
1976—Hall of Fame for
Men's Wear
1976—Return Award
(women's wear)
1977—Hall of Fame
(women's wear)
1973—Neiman-Marcus
Award

No formal design training; took business courses at night at the College of the City of New York while working days selling ties at Brooks Brothers, then as an assistant buyer for Allied Stores. Started designing neckties for Beau Brummel, with a separate division named Polo, innovating wide ties made by hand in expensive fabrics. Established Polo by Ralph Lauren as a separate company in 1968, producing a total wardrobe for men. Introduced women's clothes in 1971, beginning with cotton shirts; expanded the following year into a complete Ralph Lauren ready-to-wear collection. Polo boys' wear followed; luggage and fragrances for men and women were introduced in 1978; in 1979, Polo Western Wear, a moderately priced collection of Western apparel for men and women.

Both men's and women's apparel are licensed for manufacture in Canada and Japan. Design commit-

136

ments for men range from a jewelry collection for Tiffany to eyeglass frames, from robes to swimwear to a less expensive line called "Chaps." Among those for women are furs, shoes, scarves.

In addition to all this, he has done film work, designing for the leading men in *The Great Gatsby* in 1973, for Woody Allen and Diane Keaton in *Annie Hall* in 1977. Two uniform projects were scheduled in 1978, one for TWA, the other for the Cosmos soccer team.

Lauren chose the name "Polo," first for ties, then for men's wear, as a symbol of discreet elegance, of men who chose expensive, classic clothes and wore them with style. The same blend of essentially classic silhouettes, superb fabrics and workmanship has been applied to his women's apparel, to which he has added

 1979

1976

137

feminine dresses, a witty use of American frontier themes. For both women and men, the attitude is well bred, confident, with an offhand luxury. Definitely investment caliber, the clothes are known for excellent quality and high prices.

Lauren keeps his personal life low-key, spends it with his family—jogging in Central Park, playing tennis, on active weekends in East Hampton.

Leal, Ron (Roland)

(American designer)

BORN: Hanford, California,
23 April 1944.

Educated University of California at Santa Barbara; attended American Academy of Dramatic Arts, 1969 to 1971. Worked in Italy for Walter Albini, 1972 to 1973; Leal, Inc. Design Studio, 1975 to 1977; since 1977 designer for Betty Hanson & Co., Inc.

Leal's clothes are primarily sophisticated sportswear and evening separates to collect and add to each year. His ideal is a self-assured customer who adapts current fashion to her needs rather than following fads.

He enjoys travel and reading, likes to draw.

Maxwell, Vera

(American designer)

BORN: New York City,
22 April 1903.

AWARDS:
1951—Coty American
Fashion Critics' Special
Award (coats and suits)
1955—Neiman-Marcus
Award

Parents were Viennese; Vera was educated mainly through travel, by her parents and grandparents, and by reading. Studied ballet five years; modeled in a wholesale house where she learned clothes construction, learned to sketch, designed and made clothes for herself and other models. Studied tailoring on a visit to London where she admired and was influenced by the ease of men's clothes. Returned to United States and worked with sportswear and coat houses, Adler and Adler and Max Millstein. Vera Maxwell Originals established in 1947.

Still active today, Maxwell is one of a small group of craftsman-designers of the 1930s and 1940s, true originals who worked independently of Paris. Her specialties are simple, timeless clothes—go-together separates in fine Scottish tweeds, wool jersey, raw silk, Indian embroideries, Ultra-Suede®.

She is proud of numerous innovations including the weekend wardrobe, 1935; fencing suit, 1940 (inspired by a Hussar's uniform she saw in Vienna at age 10); warworkers' clothes under the fabric-restricting L85 rules; print dresses matched to print-lined coats; and more recently, the speed dress with a print stole, stretch-nylon top and full skirt of polyester knit, no zippers, no buttons, no hooks. In 1978, at 75 still running her own business as she had for thirty years, she dreamed of designing ". . . for a very large company that can make good clothes in good fabrics at reasonable prices."

For recreation she enjoys music, especially opera, likes ice skating, swimming, and "teaching manners to my grandchildren." She was honored in 1970 with a retrospective show at the Smithsonian Institution in Washington D.C. In 1978, a party and show were given at the Museum of the City of New York to celebrate her 75th birthday and her 50th year as a designer.

McFadden, Mary

(American designer)

BORN: 1936.

AWARDS:
Coty American Fashion
Critics' Award:
1976—"Winnie"
1978—Return Award
1979—Neiman-Marcus
Award

Raised on a cotton plantation in Memphis, Tennessee; after her father's death moved to her mother's family home in Westbury, Long Island. Graduated from Foxcroft School, Virginia in 1956; studied design at Traphagen School of Fashion in New York, in France at École Lubec and the Sorbonne. Returned to United States in 1959; studied sociology at Columbia University; took night courses at New School for Social Research. In 1962, director of public relations for CHRISTIAN DIOR-New York.

Married DeBeers executive Philip Harari, moved to South Africa in 1964. Became editor of *Vogue* South Africa which closed a year later; wrote travel columns for the *Rand Daily Mail*, contributed articles to French and American *Vogue*. In 1968 married Frank McEwen, head of Rhodes National Gallery in Salisbury, Rhodesia. While living in Rhodesia she founded a sculpture workshop called "Vokutu" for native artists;

the sculptures produced there have been shown in Paris and at The Museum of Modern Art in New York.

In 1970 McFadden returned to the United States where she worked as special projects editor for *Vogue*. Three tunics she had designed of unusual silks found in Africa and China attracted the attention of other *Vogue* editors and were shown in the magazine as a new direction. They were then bought by Henri Bendel. Her first separates were made in a tiny East 80s basement on a single sewing machine but they had the qualities that became the hallmarks of her style. The silks were hand-painted using various methods of resist techniques, colorations were oriental in feeling, calligraphy and negative spacing set them apart.

Mary McFadden, Inc. was established in 1976. In addition to the very high-priced, luxurious clothes, there is a jewelry line, a perfume was introduced in spring 1979. Other commitments include upholstery fabrics, wall hangings and wallpapers, blouses for the Alice Stuart division of Jonathan Logan.

Unique fabrics in exotic colorings, extensive use of quilting and fine pleating, ropes wrapping the figure —these are some recurring themes of McFadden's intensely individual style. Her first inspiration was drawn from ethnic themes and she concentrated mainly on poetic evening designs, rich, severe, even strange. She has since developed a more worldly and wearable approach with increasing attention to daytime clothes. Her jewelry, usually motivated by archaic symbols, is made of hand-forged brass flashed with twenty-two karat gold, combined with semi-precious stones, ceramics, macramé. All her work shares the same original point of view, refined and sophisticated.

McFadden might be considered her own best model. She is small, extremely elegant, her appearance highly stylized, from makeup to black hair worn severely straight and center-parted. While fragile looking, she is a dynamo, hard working, supremely well organized.

1976

Muto, Anthony

(American designer)

BORN: Chicago, Illinois.

Son of Italian tailor; started working with his father at age 12. Studied at Chicago Academy of Fine Arts. Designed sportswear then went to Europe for two years, working there in the couture. Returned to New York; designed for Arkay Juniors, Devonshire; in 1971 formed Marita by Anthony Muto, specializing in after-five and special occasion clothes at moderate prices.

Narducci, Leo

(American designer)

BORN: Brockton, Massachusetts.

AWARDS:
1965—Coty American Fashion Critics' Joint Special Award for "Young Contemporaries" design
1971—Print Council of America's "Tommy" Award

Son of clothing contractors; raised in Brockton. Graduated Rhode Island School of Design in 1960, with honors. Worked four years for Loomtogs, then for Gotham Originals and Guy D; formed his own company in 1967, which eventually was taken over by Puritan Fashions. In 1975 formed his own business with two partners.

His "Sportingside" collection concentrates on easy separates at moderate prices; his dress designing is concerned mainly with evening and at-home.

Licensing extends from Vogue Patterns to uniforms for National Car Rental and Holiday Inn, to a Canadian ready-to-wear manufacturer to Narducci denim jeans and skirts.

Narducci serves on the advisory board of the Laboratory Institute of Merchandising in New York, as a critic at Parsons School of Design and the Rhode Island School of Design.

Olive, Frank

(American hat designer)

BORN: Milwaukee, Wisconsin.

Graduated from Layton School of Art and Hade Fashion School in Milwaukee; studied art in Chicago before going to California to try costume design, where he worked for a few years for a San Francisco company called Dance Art. Came to New York in early 1950s hoping to design for the stage; sketches were seen by NORELL who thought Olive would be good at hats. He apprenticed with Chanda, sold fabrics in a fabric shop, worked in the Tatiana custom hat department at Saks Fifth Avenue and then for Emme.

Olive's first boutique was on MacDougal Street in Greenwich Village, "La Boutique," where he designed hats and clothes. He still does boutique items such as blouses, totes, beachwear, accessories, in addition to his three major hat collections: Olive Branch, hat bar; Frank's Girl, moderately priced; Frank Olive, the designer label. In addition, he has a Signature Collection, the equivalent of a custom operation, for women who want something different.

Even through the 1960s, when hat makers "had everything going against them," Olive worked with Seventh Avenue designers on hats for their collections and also had fashionable customers who considered a hat a necessary part of their total appearance. He says he has "never made 'millinery' . . . always made hats that make women pretty," hats that balanced the look and worked for the moment. In the late 1970s he noted a reaction against the 1960s mood of non-dress. The majority of his customers are young, care how they look, and put themselves together with a great sense of style.

1979

(Courtesy of Frank Olive)

142

Parnis, Mollie

(American designer)

BORN: New York City,
1905.

Went to work in a blouse showroom shortly after high school and was soon designing. In 1933, opened ready-to-wear firm Parnis-Livingston with husband Leon Livingston, a textile designer; went on to become one of the most successful businesswomen on Seventh Avenue, heading what has grown to be a multi-million dollar enterprise.

Parnis couture specializes in flattering, feminine dresses and ensembles for the well-to-do woman over thirty, emphasizing becomingness in beautiful fabrics, a conservative interpretation of current trends. The boutique collection was for many years designed by Morty Sussman until his death in 1979, following the same principles but with a moderate price tag. The Mollie Robert collection aimed at the working woman was begun in 1979.

Parnis administers her business; with her design staff plans and edits the couture, boutique and at-home collections; supervises selling and promotion.

She is a noted hostess, entertaining politicians, actors, artists in a beautiful apartment hung with her collection of Impressionist paintings. She has been honored for her civic contributions, such as the small parks she has donated to New York City and to Jerusalem.

Peretti, Elsa

(Jewelry designer)

BORN: Florence, Italy,
1 May 1940.

AWARDS:
1971—Coty American
Fashion Critics' Special
Award (jewelry)
1978—Award for
outstanding contribution
to the cultured pearl
industry of America and
Japan

Daughter of well-to-do Roman family. Educated at Volbicela School in Rome; took diploma in interior design; worked for a Milanese architect. In 1961 she went to Switzerland, then moved on to London where she started modeling, was seen by models' agent Wilhelmina, who suggested that Peretti come to New York. There she worked for a handful of top houses —HALSTON and OSCAR DE LA RENTA were her best clients.

In 1969 Peretti designed a few pieces of silver jewelry which Halston and GIORGIO DI SANT'ANGELO showed with their collections. These witty objects—a heart-shaped buckle, pendants in the form of small

Elsa Peretti, 1979

vases, a silver urn pendant that holds a fresh flower—were soon joined by the silver horse buckle on a long leather belt and other designs in horn, ebony and ivory. She began working with Tiffany & Co. in 1974, the first time in twenty-five years the company had carried silver jewelry.

A true international, Peretti maintains offices in Barcelona and New York, studios in San Martivel, Spain and in New York, has gone to the Orient to study semi-precious stones. Prototypes for her silver and ivory designs are made by artisans in Barcelona and the crystal pieces are done in Germany. She has continued to innovate and to be copied—a small, open, slightly lopsided heart pendant that slides on a chain is one example, diamonds-by-the-yard is another. She designed the containers for Halston's fragrance and cosmetic lines.

Peretti is tall, lean, dark-haired, wears clothes beautifully, preferring Halston and, before his death, CHARLES JAMES. She is influenced by a love of nature and inspired by Japanese designs, finds the general public her ideal customer. A perfume is slated for release in 1979.

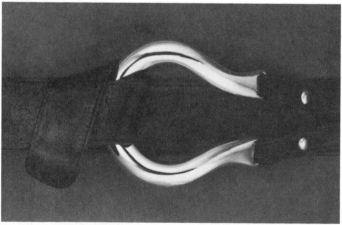

Sterling silver horseshoe buckle (Courtesy of Tiffany & Co.)

Rompollo, Dominic

(American designer)

BORN: Detroit, Michigan,
24 January 1938.

Parents were Sicilian-born immigrants and ran a small grocery store where Rompollo found ample supplies of butcher paper on which to make drawings. Went to Cass Technical High School in Detroit; worked in display design studio of J. L. Hudson Co.; attended School of Arts and Crafts while teaching ballroom dancing at night to earn money. Spent two years in service in Korea; on his return to the United States, enrolled at Parsons School of Design. Graduated in 1964 with three Golden Thimble Awards out of the four given; became assistant to GEOFFREY BEENE; designed for Teal Traina. In 1970 formed partnership in Damian Couture, closed in 1974; worked for a year doing custom clothes; in 1976 opened Dominic Rompollo, Inc. Has done signature collections for Royal Robes.

Rompollo specializes in soft, easy clothes in the middle price range; his evening clothes, especially, show flowing movement and sophisticated glamour in matte and thin wool jerseys. He designed the dress Rosalynn Carter wore to her husband's swearing-in ceremony as well as other pieces in her inaugural wardrobe.

Rompollo lives on Manhattan's East Side; enjoys opera, theater, jazz and good wines; still is devoted to dancing.

Ruffin, Clovis

(American designer)

Born: Clovis, New Mexico.

AWARDS:
1973—Coty American
Fashion Critics' Special
Award

Father was an aviator, mother in show business. Led life of army brat at boarding school and with relatives in the United States and Europe until 1960, when he went to live with his mother in New York. Has always sewn and made clothes. Started designing by drawing clothes on brown paper bags, hanging them on the wall then adding his mother's accessories. Went to Columbia University and the Sorbonne but always wanted to work at design. Formed Ruffinwear Ltd. in 1972, now a part of the Kreisler Group; also designs the Clovis dress collection, mostly late-day, plus handbags, travel kits, loungewear.

His design philosophy is glamour with practicality—pull-on, snap-on, wrap-on clothes that go anywhere, anytime—combining simple cut with elegance in a moderate-price bracket.

Sachs, Gloria

(American designer)

BORN: Scarsdale, New York.

Graduated from Skidmore College, fine arts major. Did graduate work at Cranbrook Academy of Art near Detroit, where her involvement in textiles began. First worked as a fabric designer, often dyeing her own yarns. Used first earnings to finance a year in Europe; painted in the atelier of Léger in Paris; worked with Italian architects, Gio Ponti and France Albini. Returned to New York, deciding to work in textiles but went to work in Bloomingdale's in the decorating department; became fashion coordinator for the store. Married to Irwin Sachs; two children. After the birth of her children, she joined Saks Fifth Avenue as a designer, with such success that in 1970 she was able to open her own firm on Seventh Avenue.

Sachs's studies as painter, sculptor and hand-weaver are influential in her work. She is noted for beautiful fabrics in unusual prints, colors and texture combinations, and for lithe, flowing shapes, very simple and well-cut. Her clothes are in the better price range.

Sanchez, Fernando

(American designer specializing in lingerie and furs)

BORN: Spain

AWARDS:
Coty American Fashion
Critics' Award:
1974, 1977—Special
Award (lingerie)
1975—Special Award for
fur design (for Revillon)

Son of Spanish father, Belgian mother. Was prize winner in same International Wool Secretariat competition in which SAINT LAURENT won an award; both went on to the house of CHRISTIAN DIOR, where Sanchez designed lingerie, accessories, sweaters, for the Dior European boutiques. First came to New York to do the Dior American lingerie line and for several years commuted between Paris and New York, doing several collections here. At the same time began designing furs for Revillon; worked for them for twelve years in Paris and New York, becoming known for

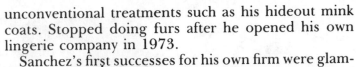

unconventional treatments such as his hideout mink coats. Stopped doing furs after he opened his own lingerie company in 1973.

Sanchez's first successes for his own firm were glamorous lace-trimmed silk gowns, to which he added camisole tops, boxer shorts, bikini pants. He went on to develop lingerie on the separates principle, mixing colors, lengths and fabrics to make a modern look. He calls his designs "home clothes," although many styles can also be worn on the beach or for dancing, has worked out a similar plan for men. His lingerie is seductive, luxurious, trend-setting and expensive; he is given credit for reviving interest in extravagant underthings.

He divides his free time between his three residences—a house in Morocco, a place in Paris, his New York loft.

1975

Sant'Angelo, Giorgio
(Giorgio di Sant'Angelo)

(American designer)

BORN: Florence, Italy,
5 May 1939.

AWARDS:
Coty American Fashion
Critics' Award:
1968—Special Award
1970—"Winnie"

Spent childhood in South America and Italy; studied law; trained as industrial designer and architect; later studied with Picasso before coming to the United States in 1962 to work with Walt Disney.

In 1963 worked in New York as textile designer and stylist for design studios and volume fabric houses; at same time was free lance designer-consultant on environmental projects and for E.I. du Pont de Nemours on experiments with Lucite as a material for the home,

1977

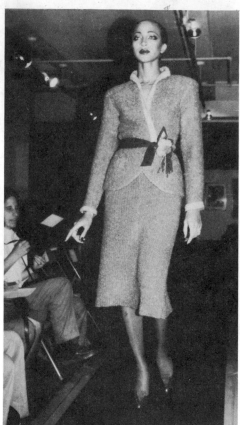

1979

also designing fashion accessories which received extensive and favorable press coverage. Founded Sant' Angelo Ready-to-Wear in 1966; and in 1968, di Sant' Angelo, Inc.

Sant'Angelo's first fashion success was with his accessories; he went on to do gypsy dresses and modern patchwork clothes, knitwear, ready-to-wear, leathers. In the late 1970s he remains very much an individualist, interested in new uses for materials such as stretch fabrics incorporating spandex, and designing for those who like their clothes a little out of the ordinary. He has also done costumes for two films featuring Tamara Dobson as Cleopatra Jones.

In 1978 his licensing covers women's ready-to-wear, swimwear, lingerie, sportswear, furs, men's wear, carpets, furniture; he maintains a couture operation for a roster of celebrity customers. He has said, "I like to do absolutely everything because one area always brings ideas for another."

Scaasi, Arnold (born Arnold Isaacs)

(American couturier)

BORN: Montreal, Canada, 1931.

AWARDS:
1958—Coty American Fashion Critics' "Winnie"
1959—Neiman-Marcus Award

Son of a furrier. After high school lived in Melbourne, Australia with an aunt who dressed at CHANEL and SCHIAPARELLI and influenced him with her disciplined approach to dress and living. Began studying art in Australia; returned to Montreal to study couture; designed clothes for private clients and saved enough money to go to Paris to complete his fashion studies at the Chambre Syndicale. Traveled in Europe for a year, then went to PAQUIN in Paris as an apprentice.

Returned to New York in 1955; worked as a sketcher for a couture house; designed coats and suits for a Seventh Avenue manufacturer. In 1957, on a shoestring, he opened his own wholesale business and in 1960 bought and renovated a Manhattan town house for his ready-to-wear presentations; discontinued ready-to-wear and switched to couture in 1963. He has also designed costume jewelry, men's ties, sweaters, furs for Ben Kahn and Ritter Brothers. One of the last of the true custom designers in the United States, he is known for spectacular evening wear in luxurious fabrics, often trimmed with furs or feathers.

Lives in an apartment overlooking Central Park; has a weekend house on Long Island; vacations in foreign cities; collects twentieth-century art.

Schlumberger, Jean

(Designer of jewelry and art objects)

BORN: 1907.

AWARDS:
1958—Coty American Fashion Critics' Special Award (the first ever given for jewelry)
1977—Made Chevalier of the National Order of Merit of France

Son of Alsatian textile magnate. Sent to America in his teens to work in a New Jersey silk factory; returned to France, abandoned textile business, took job with an art publishing firm. Became part of the inventive Paris world of fashion, art and society.

First jewelry designs were clips made from china flowers found in the Paris Flea Market. These pieces brought him to the attention of ELSA SCHIAPARELLI who commissioned him to design costume jewelry. He progressed to gold and precious stones, attracting a prominent international clientele, including the Duchess of Windsor.

Went into the army at the advent of World War II;

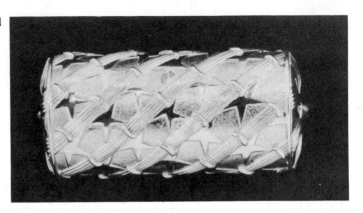

Stars and Stripes, 18K-gold cigarette box (Courtesy of Tiffany & Co.)

Platinum and 18K-gold pavé diamond bird stands on top of a citrine rock

PUBLICATIONS:
  Two-volume set of art books devoted to his works published in a limited edition in 1977 by Franco Maria Ricci, Milan and Paris

was evacuated from Dunkirk to England; came to the United States and designed clothes for Chez Ninon, opened an office on Fifth Avenue with his partner, Nicolas Bongard. Rejoined the Free French and served in the Near East; returned to New York in 1946 and opened a salon on East 63rd Street. In 1956 joined Tiffany & Co., where he is currently a vice president. A special elevator takes clients to his salon on the mezzanine of the New York store.

Schlumberger has been equated with Fabergé and Cellini. His virtuosity, imagination and skill bring forth exuberant fantasies: A sunflower of gold, emeralds, diamonds, with a 100 carat sapphire heart, planted in a clay pot set in a gold cachepot; snowpea clips of malachite and gold; moss-covered shells dripping with diamond dew. He works as an artist, using enamel and stones as if they were paint, has revived Renaissance techniques such as enamel work and the custom of mixing semiprecious stones with diamonds. His work has been the subject of a lecture at the Metropolitan Museum of Art; a loan exhibition of jewelry and objects was presented in 1961 by the Wildenstein Gallery, New York.

He travels extensively, especially to exotic and tropical places, divides the rest of his time between Paris, New York and his house in Guadeloupe.

Selwyn, Harriet

(American designer)

BORN: Brooklyn, New York,
18 January 1931.

AWARDS:
1977—Lord & Taylor
Creative Designer Award
MEMBER:
Board of Directors, F.I.T.C.,
Los Angeles

1976

Graduated Midwood High School, 1949. Did office work briefly, free-lanced as a fur model; in 1950 went to work for a sweater manufacturer who ". . . taught me a lot about the nuances of the business and selling in a volume market." Spent nearly twenty years in the garment district as showroom model, sales manager, stylist, public relations person. In 1968 began designing and making jewelry; moved to Los Angeles with her adopted daughter in 1971; formed a partnership with another transplanted New Yorker in a jewelry firm called Fragments. They soon expanded into clothing.

Selwyn's first success was a chiffon "sweater," an idea given her by her friend WILLI SMITH. In 1973 she added a surplice top; in 1974 evolved the idea of the complete "Fragments" wardrobe and also the way to sell it. The designs are simple, usually of Qiana nylon jersey in solid colors, one size to fit just about any figure. A tent dress, drawstring pants, surplice tops with long or short sleeves, a peasant blouse, etc., go on forwards or backwards, intermix in countless groupings. She has since developed deluxe and glamorous clothes in pale silks, prints, plaids, stripes, to be worn by themselves or with the basic Fragments components.

She has overcome personal disaster—a mastectomy and the death of her daughter in 1975—to go on and expand her ideas and consolidate her position as a leader in the thriving young California design movement.

Shields, Alexander

(American men's wear designer)

BORN: San Francisco,
California, 21 October 1921.

Educated California Institute of Technology; Georgetown University School of Foreign Service. Established Alexander Shields, Inc. in 1947 as a wholesale and retail operation with his own shop on Park Avenue, individual shops in specialty stores across the country. Designed tennis wear for Jockey International from 1973 to 1978; has a cologne and soap under his own label.

Shields is given credit for bringing new freedom to men's attire with comfortable, colorful, casual clothes within a traditional framework—jersey-knit suits, kimonos, fly-front shirts, caftans.

He plays tennis for recreation and is nationally ranked in the 55 years and over category; is active in a number of groups devoted to American history and the American heritage.

Sibley, Joan (Sibley-Powell)

(American designer)

BORN: Gipsy, Pennsylvania,
    1 August 1941.

AWARDS:
    1975—Gold Coast Award,
    Chicago
MEMBER:
    New York Council of
    Fashion Designers

Studied fashion design at Moore College of Art in Philadelphia; on graduation was awarded a European Traveling Fellowship. She traveled extensively in Europe, studied at the Sorbonne, absorbed the European aura of elegance and taste. With fellow Moore student launched firm Sibley-Coffee, 1968; name changed to Sibley, 1977.

Sibley clothes combine European ideas of fit, fine fabrics and femininity with an American insistence on comfort, naturalness and color, influenced by modern young women like the designer. Mostly suits and evening wear, they unite classic simplicity and understatement with sexiness and a sense of luxury and glamour; are noted for refined finish and couture touches. They are in the better to deluxe price range.

The designer is married to film producer Peter Powell. She enjoys entertaining and loves going out; her favorite recreation is watching her son play.

Simpson, Adele

(American designer)

BORN: New York City,
    8 December 1903.

AWARDS:
    1946—Neiman-Marcus
    Award

Graduated from Wadleigh High School, New York; began designing at 17, attending Pratt Institute at night. In 1925 went to work for Ben Gershel & Co., a maker of coats and suits; designed for William Bass Company, 1930 to 1934; Mary Lee Frocks, 1934 to 1944; Adele Simpson, Inc., founded in 1944.

The Simpson clothes have always been intended for conservative women with discerning taste, are pretty

1947—Coty American
  Fashion Critics' "Winnie"
1953—First National Cotton
  Award
EXHIBITION:
  Honored by the Fashion
  Institute of Technology at
  reception in November
  1978, and with exhibit
  "100 Treasures of
  Design," items collected
  by Adele and Wesley
  Simpson
MEMBER:
  The Fashion Group

and feminine in delicate colors and prints
coordinated into complete wardrobes. She
comfort and function as well as beauty, is k
excellent quality and fine workmanship. In the late
1970s, with designer Donald Hopson, a somewhat
younger, more fluid look was introduced.

A tiny woman, less than five feet tall, Simpson is a
dedicated traveler, has made four trips around the
world, amassing a notable collection of costumes,
dolls, fabrics and fashion-related books, which she has
now given to the Fashion Institute of Technology. Her
life, centered around her family, is divided between
her business, her Manhattan apartment and her Connecticut country house, where she enjoys gardening.
She was married for forty-four years to Wesley Simpson, a textile manufacturer, who died in 1976. Her
son, Jeffrey, has his own apparel business; her daughter Joan and son-in-law Richard Raines assist Mrs.
Simpson in hers.

Smith, Willi

(American designer)

BORN: Philadelphia,
  Pennsylvania.

Studied fashion illustration at the Philadelphia Museum College of Art, 1964. Arrived in New York in
1965 with two scholarships to Parsons School of Design, one from the Philadelphia Board of Education,
the other from Parsons. Free-lanced as a sketcher
while in school; left Parsons in 1968 to work for a knit
house; first design job was at Glenora, a junior sportswear firm. In 1969 was first designer for Digits, a
sportswear firm. In 1976 Willi Wear Ltd. was established with Smith as vice president and designer; Willi
Wear Men was introduced in 1978 "to bridge the gap
between jeans and suits."

One of the young black designers who came to the
fore in the late 1960s, Smith is slender, young-look-
ing, gentle in manner, hard working. His innovative,
spirited clothes are in the moderate-price range, fun
to wear as well as functional, keep their feeling from
one year to another so that pieces from new collections mix comfortably with those from previous years.
He prefers natural fibers because of their comfort and
utility, designs his own textiles and goes to India several times a year to supervise the collections.

Smith has done a lingerie collection for Henri Bendel, textiles for Bedford Stuyvesant Design Works, furniture for Knoll International; designs for Butterick Patterns since 1972.

1978

Willi Smith, 1978

Stavropoulos, George

(American designer)

BORN: Greece.

Studied dress design in Paris. Had custom house in Athens, 1949 to 1960; married Greek-American working for American Embassy in Athens; came to New York in 1961, opening his business on West 57th Street. Now is engaged in making luxury ready-to-wear sold through fine specialty stores, some custom work for special private customers.

While he designs a complete day-to-evening collection, Stavropoulos is primarily recognized for exceptional late-day and evening clothes in soft materials—crepe, jersey, chiffon—is considered a master of draping. His clothes are in the deluxe price bracket, classically simple shapes, exquisitely made in luxurious fabrics.

Suppon, Charles

(American designer)

BORN: Collinsville, Illinois,
12 January 1949.

AWARDS:
1978—Coty American
Fashion Critics' "Winnie"
MEMBER:
Council of Fashion
Designers of America

Attended School of the Art Institute, University of Chicago, 1967 to 1971, earned B.F.A. Worked from 1971 to 1976 as assistant to CALVIN KLEIN; since then has been designer for Intre Sport, doing clothes for women and men, "all-American sportswear for many moods and occasions." Outside commitments include Simplicity Designer Patterns, fall 1977; Japanese licensing for men and women, spring 1979.

Suppon likes to treat conventional fabrics in unconventional ways—quilting corduroy, lining a sweater with pieced fox, making a blazer from snakeskin. He also designs furs, plans to add evening clothes and swimsuits. Clothes are in the better price range.

Finds relaxation at the theater and movies and at concerts.

Sylbert, Viola

(American designer)

BORN: New York City.

AWARDS:
1975—Coty American
Fashion Critics' Special
Award for fur design (for
Alixandre)

Daughter of a dress manufacturer. Took M.A. degree in retailing at New York University. Her first love was writing, her second love theatrical costume design; as a more secure way to earn a living she took a job as fashion coordinator at Ohrbach's. There she kept offering suggestions to improve the merchandise, gradually worked into designing with her first success coming in leathers. Around 1965, recognizing that "I'm not a 9 to 5 person," she began to free-lance, which she has done ever since. She enjoys the stimulation of working with different people on different kinds of projects, which can run the gamut from designs for Columbia-Minerva hand-knitting yarns to furs for Alixandre.

In 1970, when Alixandre was looking for ready-to-wear designers to bring a fresh approach to their furs, Gerry Stutz of Henri Bendel, a store with which Sylbert has had close associations, suggested Sylbert and another designer. The other designer is gone, Sylbert is still doing two collections a year for Alixandre. In addition, she has designed two "trend collections" (1976–77 and 1978–79) for The Wool Bureau which include jersey dresses and men's sweaters; sweaters

1970

for Peter G's General Store, a division of Sportwhirl; raincoats for Beged Or. She will also be getting back to her first love as she has contracted to write a book telling "all the things you've always wanted to know about furs."

She does most of her sketching and research at home with the help of two assistants, travels to Europe and Hong Kong several times a year. She feels that the most important influence on clothes today is life style, "something so obvious it's not worth mentioning."

Tassell, Gustave (Gus)

(*American designer*)

BORN: Philadelphia, Pennsylvania, c. 1927.

AWARDS:
1959—International Silk Association

Studied at Pennsylvania Academy of Fine Arts. Did window displays for HATTIE CARNEGIE; had small couture business in Philadelphia; was designer at Carnegie but left in 1952 to spend two years in Paris, where he supported himself by selling sketches to couture houses. In 1959, started his own ready-to-wear business in Los Angeles.

Tassell was a friend of NORELL, sharing with him a sure sense of proportion, an insistence on simplicity of line and refined detail, a subtle use of color. Became design head of Norman Norell, Inc. after Norell's death in 1972, a position he held until the firm closed. In 1976, he signed to do furs for Michael Forrest.

Tice, Bill

(American designer specializing in robes and loungewear)

BORN: Indiana, 1946.

AWARDS:
1974—Coty American
Fashion Critics' Special
Award (lingerie)

Majored in fashion design at the University of Cincinnati where he entered a work-study program, doing everything from selling fishing tackle to designing window displays. Came to New York in the mid 1960s; designed for a number of ready-to-wear firms.

In 1968 he became designer for Royal Robes where he introduced such key at-home ideas as the jersey

1969

1976

float, the quilted gypsy look, closely pleated caftans. In 1974 designed for Sayour; moved to Swirl in 1975. Here he has produced widely imitated fleece robes, innovative and salable loungewear—from sundresses to printed sarongs to quilted silk coats and narrow pants. He designs domestic linens for Bloomcraft.

Tice is known as a perfectionist who truly loves loungewear. He does a great many personal appearances to "keep me realistic about fashion"; feels that the way people live has changed, making possible the whole idea of "pleasurewear"—casual loungewear that can go out of the house.

Tiffeau, Jacques

(Franco-American designer)

BORN: Chenevelles, France, 1927.

AWARDS:
Coty American Fashion
Critics Award:
1960—"Winnie"
1964—Return Award
1966—Neiman-Marcus
Award

Trained with men's tailors in Chenevelles and Paris; career interrupted by war service; came to New York in 1952. Studied nights at Art Students League and trained under friend CHRISTIAN DIOR while also working as patternmaker for Monte Sano & Pruzan. In 1958, he and Beverly Pruzan Busch established Tiffeau-Busch Inc., making young, high-spirited clothes in the middle price range. Since the firm closed, Tiffeau has worked for Saint Laurent, Originala, Blassport.

He is an excellent tailor, an inventive designer of modern, sporty, sexy clothes, uncluttered and witty. In addition to ready-to-wear, he has designed swimsuits for Catalina.

Tilley, Monika

(American designer)

BORN: Vienna, Austria, 25 July 1934.

AWARDS:
1975—Coty American
Fashion Critics' Special
Award (swimsuits)

Grew up in Austria and England; took M.A. degree from Academy of Applied Arts, Vienna, in 1956; came to the United States in 1957. Head designer for White Stag and Cole of California's Sportswear Division, 1960 to 1967; associated with Anne Klein Studio, Mallory Leathers and Elon of California, 1968 to 1970. In 1970 she incorporated as Monika Tilley Limited; designs swim and beachwear for Elon, children's swim things for Suntogs, at-home and bedroom fashions for Miss Elaine.

1976—Print Council of
America's "Tommy"
Award (twice in same year,
once for beach clothes and
sportswear, once for
loungewear and lingerie
"for her original designs
and use of prints")

Tilley has always been involved in sports so that her sportswear designs, while fashionable and often seductive, are thoroughly functional. In swimwear she has used bias cuts, cotton madras shirred with elastic, a technique of angling the weave of a fabric so that it shapes the body as it covers it.

She relaxes with active sports—skiing, riding, swimming, sailing—designs for people "who like themselves well enough to be fashionable."

1973

Trigère, Pauline

(American designer)

BORN: Paris, France,
   4 November 1912.

AWARDS:
   1950—Neiman-Marcus
      Award
   Coty American Fashion
      Critics' Award:
      1949—"Winnie"
      1951—Return Award
      1959—Hall of Fame
   1972—Silver Medal of the
      City of Paris

Daughter of a dressmaker and a tailor. Studied at Victor Hugo College in Paris. Learned to cut and fit in her father's shop; made her first muslins there. Came to New York with her brother Robert, her husband, and her two infant sons in 1932, en route to Chile, liked what she saw and stayed on. Worked at Ben Gershel & Co.; became assistant designer at HATTIE CARNEGIE; in 1942 opened her own business with a collection of eleven styles.

Trigère does not sketch but cuts and drapes directly from the bolt, notably coats, capes, suits, dresses, in luxurious fabrics, unusual tweeds, and prints. The deceptive simplicity of the clothes stems from artistic, intricate cut, especially flattering to the mature figure. Today the Trigère name appears on scarves, jewelry, furs, men's ties, sunglasses, bedroom fashions, paperworks and servingware; her fragrance was introduced in 1973.

Accomplished cook and hostess, passionate gardener, avid concert- and theater-goer. Trigère does most of the designing for her firm, is aided in the business by her older son, Jean-Pierre Radley. The younger son, Philippe, teaches Russian language and literature.

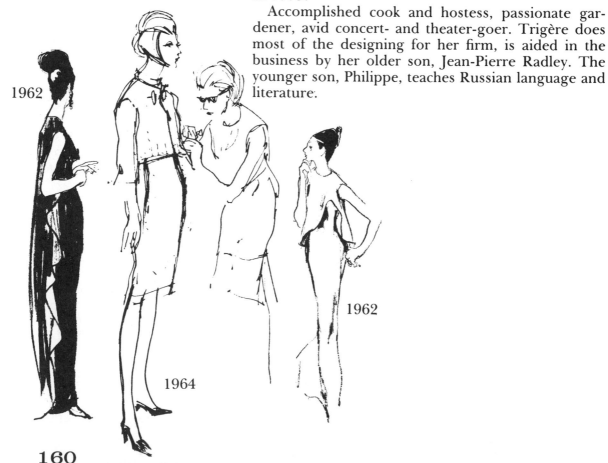

1962

1962

1964

Van den Akker, Koos

(Fashion designer)

BORN: Holland

1976

Quit school in 1950 to work at design. Started making dresses when just 11 years old; entered Netherlands Royal Academy of Art at 15, stayed three years. Worked in department stores in The Hague and in Paris; enrolled at L'Ecole Guerre Lavigne in Paris where he completed a two-year fashion program in seven months. Apprenticed at CHRISTIAN DIOR; returned to The Hague where he spent six years selling custom-made dresses in his own boutique.

In August 1968 came to New York with very little money and a portable sewing machine; set up his "office" by the fountain at Lincoln Center and took commissions from passers-by. One customer introduced him to Eve Stillman who gave him a job designing lingerie. Opened his own boutique on West 72nd Street, selling to other boutiques and to Henri Bendel. Moved to Madison Avenue in 1975; opened a second shop in Beverly Hills, 1978.

Van den Akker designs everything from lingerie to day and evening clothes. He specializes in simply cut shapes in beautiful fabrics with his signature "collages," insets of colorful prints and lace. His clothes are considered collector's items and have been on display in the Museum of Contemporary Crafts. Customers include Cher, Madeleine Kahn, Elizabeth Taylor, Gloria Vanderbilt.

"My theory of fashion is simple: I just want to make pretty clothes. . . . There is no fad in my clothes; in two years or in ten, I will still be doing what *I* want to do . . ."

Vass, Joan

(American designer)

BORN: New York City,
   19 May 1925.

AWARDS:
   June 1978—"Extraordinary
   Women in Fashion,"
   Smithsonian Institution,
   Washington, D.C.

Attended Vassar College, graduated from University of Wisconsin as philosophy major; did graduate work in area of aesthetics at University of Buffalo and The New School of Social Research, New York City. Was curator at Museum of Modern Art; editor at Harry N. Abrams, publishers of art books. No fashion design training. Married to Gene Vass; four children.

Established business, 1973, incorporated, 1977; now has a living loft and workshop where some of the

1978

clothes are made; others are made by the workers in their own homes.

Vass is best known for crochets and handmade or handloomed knits and for imaginative, functional clothes in simplified shapes, subtle colorings. She favors natural fibers; her aim is to make modern clothes for modern women and men; she is recognized by retailers and the press as a highly creative, original designer.

While she had always knitted and crocheted, Vass got into designing by accident in the early 1970s when two of her concerns intersected. The first was about women with salable skills but no way to market them, women who either could not work away from home or did not want to be confined in offices or factories. The second was a conviction that there was an unsatisfied need for handmade articles of good quality that could be worn and loved as long as they held together.

She found a number of older women with superb craft skills and began designing things for them to knit and crochet, selling the articles privately. At the same time, she continued to work at her editing job. The new enterprise took so much time that she wanted to give it up but was persuaded by her workers to keep on. First recognition and large order came from Henri Bendel, other stores followed.

Von Furstenberg, Diane —————————

(American ready-to-wear designer)

BORN: Brussels, Belgium.

PUBLICATIONS:
Book of Beauty. New York: Simon & Schuster, Inc., 1976.

Educated in Spain, England, Switzerland; degree in economics from University of Geneva. With husband, Egon, moved to the United States in 1969.

Decided to try designing dresses for which she saw a need, something that would feel comfortable, look chic, sell at moderate prices. First patterns were cut on her dining room table, shipped to a friend in Italy who had them made up in a factory outside Florence. In 1971, packed her first samples in a suitcase and started showing them to department store buyers. Quickly became known for lightweight jersey dresses, usually in prints, especially the wrapdress with surplice top and long sleeves.

She has gone on to produce a makeup and treatment line of cosmetics, a fragrance named "Tatiana," after her daughter. Diane Von Furstenberg, Inc. is now a division of Puritan Fashions.

Licenses include stationery, costume jewelry, loungewear, furs, handbags and small leathers, designs for Vogue Patterns, raincoats, scarves, shoes, sunglasses, table linens, wall coverings.

The designer lives in a Manhattan apartment, has a country place in Connecticut.

Wacs, Ilie

(American designer)

BORN: Vienna, Austria.

1963

When the Germans invaded Austria, Wacs's family escaped to China, the only country that admitted refugees without a visa, and lived in Shanghai until 1941 when the Japanese occupied the city and forced all refugees into a ghetto. His father, who had run one of Vienna's leading men's custom tailoring businesses, supported the family by taking old suits, stripping them and reversing them to make new garments. Wacs helped him in the work, learning the art of tailoring from the inside out.

After the 1945 liberation he earned a scholarship to study art at the École des Beaux Arts in Paris; turned to fashion and worked in the Paris couture. Was discovered and brought to New York by Philip Mangone, a leading American tailor of his day. Wacs worked for Mangone and others; had his own couture house; in 1964 joined Originala, a coat and suit firm, where he was head designer until 1972. Designed for a conglomerate under his own label for two years; acquired ownership of Ilie Wacs Inc. in 1975.

Wacs believes that good fit is synonymous with good fashion, that contemporary clothes should be uncomplicated and free of gimmicks. He is known for excellent tailoring in fine fabrics, does coats, suits and separates in the better price range. Furs were added in fall 1978.

He and his family live in New York City, have a house on Long Island where Wacs has a studio and can indulge in his favorite pastime, serious painting.

Weinberg, Chester

(American designer)

BORN: New York City

AWARDS:
1970—Coty American
Fashion Critics' "Winnie"
1972—Maison Blanche
"Rex" Award, New
Orleans

Attended High School of Music and Art, Parsons School of Design; took B.S. degree in art education at New York University. Worked for a number of years as assistant at Seventh Avenue houses before opening his own business in 1966, closed 1975. In 1978 was designing dresses and sportswear for a company backed by Jones Apparel Group; designs cashmere sweaters for men and women for Ballantyne of Scotland; also does furs. His clothes are sophisticated, classic, never exaggerated or overpowering; he is especially interested in fabrics and draws them from resources around the world.

Weinberg enjoys travel; loves to work with students and guest-teaches at Parsons and the Art Institute of Chicago; serves on the Board of Overseers at Parsons, as a jury critic in Chicago. He designed the costumes for the Twyla Tharp ballet, *As Time Goes By.*

Weitz, John

(American designer of men's and women's sportswear)

BORN: Berlin, Germany, 1923.

AWARDS:
1974—Coty American
Fashion Critics' Special
Men's Wear Award
PUBLICATIONS:
Man in Charge. New York:
Macmillan, Inc., 1974.
*Sports Clothes for Your Sports
Car.* New York: Arco
Publishing Co., Inc., 1958.
The Value of Nothing. (novel).
New York: Stein & Day
Publishers, 1970.

Educated in England; quit school and went to Paris where he apprenticed at MOLYNEUX. Arrived in the United States in 1940. Served in the United States Army; after the war met Dorothy Shaver of Lord & Taylor and showed her some of his women's sportswear designs based on men's clothes. Started licensing in 1954; raced sport cars.

He is considered a pioneer in design of practical clothes for sports and modern living. In the 1950s introduced women's sport clothes with a men's wear look, showed town pants, strapless dress over bra and shorts, etc. In the 1960s he presented so-called ready-to-wear couture, where the design could be chosen from sketches and swatches, and Contour Clothes for men inspired by jeans, cowboy jackets, fatigue coveralls. From 1970 confined apparel designing to clothes and accessories for men. In 1978 licensed name for a chain of John Weitz boutiques selling both men's wear and women's apparel. Introduced a women's sportswear collection in 1979. Products range from ice buckets to men's fragrance; a John Weitz automobile was scheduled for 1979.

Winter, Harriet
(Mrs. H. Winter of Yesterday's News)

(American designer)

1978

Daughter of an actors' agent; no formal design training. Began in fashion by reworking old clothes from her husband Lewis's collection, which they then resold, went on to make her own designs. At first her work was reminiscent of the 1930s and 1940s, gradually evolved into a thoroughly modern, completely personal style.

She feels that as fashion changes, the changes should be expressed by modern means and new constructions rather than repeating methods from the past. For example, when shoulders broaden, the effect should be accomplished by cut or draping or means other than the shoulder pads of previous eras.

Her collection includes day clothes and evening separates of the sports-evening genre—easy, contemporary, individual—for the woman who doesn't want to look exactly like everyone else.

Woods, Wayne

(American designer)

BORN: Los Angeles, California, 15 October 1951.

MEMBER:
California Contemporary Fashion Guild

Educated Crespi Carmelite High School, Loyola-Marymount University. From 1968 to 1975 design experience covers jewelry, leather and resort wear; designs for Right Bank Clothing Co. and Motherhood Maternity; freelance loungewear. Established Wayne Woods Inc., 1976.

Woods is best known for evening clothes—simple shapes in innovative fabrics, such special details as hand painting, trapunto, beading, experimental silk screening techniques. He is inspired by Chinese art and by the Impressionists; his clothes are in the better-to-designer price range.

He is a sports fan, particularly baseball and ice hockey; enjoys painting for recreation.

BIBLIOGRAPHY

Not all the listed books have contributed to this edition of Who's Who in Fashion. *This bibliography is compiled to help the reader in the study of fashion.*

Amies, Hardy. *Just So Far.* St. James Place, London: Collins, 1954.

————. *ABC of Men's Fashion.* London: Newnes, 1964.

Baillen, C. *Chanel Solitaire.* Translated by Barbara Bray. New York: Quadrangle-The NY Times Book Co., 1974.

Ballard, Bettina. *In My Fashion.* New York: David McKay Co., Inc., 1960.

Balmain, Pierre. *My Years and Success* (autobiography). Translated by E. Lanchbery and G. Young. London: Cassell & Co. Ltd., 1964. New York: Doubleday & Company, Inc., 1965.

Battersby, M. *Art Deco Fashion (Couturier's Creations 1908–12).* Academy Edition, 1974.

Beaton, Cecil. *The Glass of Fashion.* New York: Doubleday & Company, Inc., 1954.

————. *Fair Lady.* New York: Holt, Rinehart & Winston, 1964.

————. *The Years Between Diaries 1939–1944.* New York: Holt, Rinehart & Winston, 1965.

————. *Cecil Beaton: Memoirs of the 40s.* New York: McGraw-Hill Book Co., 1977.

Bender, Marylin. *Beautiful People.* New York: Coward, McCann & Geoghegan, Inc., 1967.

Blum, Stella. *Designs by Erté. Fashion Drawings & Illustrations from Harper's Bazaar.* New York: 1976.

Boucher, Francois. *20,000 Years of Fashion.* New York: Harry N. Abrams, Inc., 1967.

Brady, James. *Super Chic.* Boston: Little, Brown & Co., 1974.

Brockman, Helen L. *The Theory of Fashion Design.* New York: John Wiley & Sons Inc., 1965.

Brogden, J. *Fashion Design.* London: Studio Vista, 1971.

Byers, Margaretta. *Designing Women.* New York: Simon & Schuster, 1938.

Calasibetta, Dr. Charlotte. *Fairchild's Dictionary of Fashion.* New York: Fairchild Publications, Inc., 1975.

Charles-Roux, Edmonde. *Chanel: her life, her world, and the woman behind the legend she herself created.* France: Editions Grosset & Faquelle, 1974. Distributed by Random House, New York.

Chase, Edna Woolman and Ilka Chase. *Always in Vogue.* New York: Doubleday & Company, Inc., 1954.

Chierichetti, David. *Hollywood Costume Design.* New York: Crown Publishers, Inc., 1976.

Creed, Charles. *Maid to Measure.* London: Jarrolds, 1961.

Dache, Lilly. *Talking through My Hats.* Edited by Dorothy Roe Lewis. New York: Coward-McCann, Inc., 1946.

Davenport, Millia. *The Book of Costume.* New York: Crown Publishers, Inc., 1948.

Daves, Jessica. *Ready-Made Miracle.* New York: G.P. Putnam's Sons, 1967.

Daves, Jessica, Alexander Liberman, Bryan Holmes and Katherine Tweed. *The World in Vogue.* Compiled by The Viking Press and *Vogue* Magazine, 1963.

Dior, Christian. *Talking about Fashion.* Translated by Eugenia Sheppard. New York: G.P. Putnam's Sons, 1954.

————. *Christian Dior and I.* Translated by Antonia Fraser. New York: E.P. Dutton & Company, Inc., 1957.

_____. *Dior by Dior.* Translated by Antonia Fraser. London: Weidenfeld & Nicolson, 1957. Harmondsworth, England: Penguin Books, 1968.

Dixon, H. Vernon. *The Rag Pickers.* New York: David McKay Co., Inc., 1966.

Erté. *Erté Fashions.* New York: St. Martin's Press, 1972.

_____. *Erté—Things I Remember* (autobiography). London: Peter Owen Limited, 1975.

Ewing, Elizabeth. *History of 20th Century Fashion.* New York: Charles Scribner's Sons, 1974.

Fairchild, John. *The Fashionable Savages.* New York: Doubleday & Company, Inc., 1965.

Ferragamo, Salvatore. *Shoemaker of Dreams* (autobiography). England: George G. Harrap & Co. Ltd., 1972.

Fogarty, Anne. *Wife-Dressing.* New York: Julian Messner Inc., 1959.

Garland, Madge. *Fashion.* London: Penguin Books, 1962.

_____. *The Changing Form of Fashion.* London: J.M. Dent & Sons, 1970.

Glynn, Prudence. *In Fashion: Dress in the Twentieth Century.* New York: Oxford University Press, 1978.

Gold, Annalee. *75 Years of Fashion.* New York: Fairchild Publications, 1975.

Gorsline, Douglas Warner. *What People Wore: A Visual History of Dress from Ancient Times to 20th Century America.* New York: Viking Press, 1952.

Haedrich, Marcel. *Coco Chanel, Her Life, Her Secrets.* Boston: Little, Brown & Co., 1971.

Hartnell, Norman. *Silver and Gold* (autobiography). London: Evans Brothers, 1955.

_____. *Royal Courts of Fashion.* London: Cassell & Co. Ltd., 1971.

Hawes, Elizabeth. *Fashion Is Spinach.* New York: Random House, 1938.

Head, Edith. *Fashion As a Career.* New York: Julian Messner, 1966.

Horst. *Salute to the Thirties.* New York: Viking Press, 1971.

Howell, Georgina. *In Vogue: Six Decades of Fashion.* London: Allen Lane, 1975.

Kybalova, Ludmila, Olga Herbenova and Milena Lamorova. *The Pictorial Encyclopedia of Fashion,* 2nd ed.. Translated by Claudia Rosoux. England: Hamlyn Publishers, 1968. New York: Crown Publishers, Inc., 1969.

Lambert, Eleanor. *World of Fashion: People, Places and Resources.* New York: R.R. Bowker Company, 1976.

Langlade, Emile. *Rose Bertin: The Creator of Fashion at the Court of Marie-Antoinette.* Adapted from the French by Dr. Angelo S. Rappoport. New York: Charles Scribner's Sons, 1913.

Latour, Anny. *Kings of Fashion.* Translated by Mervyn Saville. London: Weidenfeld and Nicolson, 1958.

_____. *Paris Fashion.* London: Michael Joseph, 1972.

Laver, James. *Taste and Fashion.* London: George G. Harrap & Co. Ltd., 1937.

_____. *A Concise History of Costume.* London: Thames and Hudson, 1969.

Levin, Phyllis Lee. *The Wheels of Fashion.* New York: Doubleday & Company, Inc., 1965.

Lynam, Ruth, editor. *Couture.* New York: Doubleday & Company, Inc., 1972.

Marcus, Stanley. *Minding the Store.* Boston: Little, Brown & Co., 1974.

McCardell, Claire. *What Shall I Wear?.* New York: Simon & Schuster, 1956.

Milinaire, Caterine and Carol Troy. *Cheap Chic.* New York: Harmony Books, 1975.

Morris, Bernadine. *The Fashion Makers: An Inside Look at America's Leading Designers.* New York: Random House, 1978.

Payne, Blanche. *History of Costume: From the Ancient Egyptians to the Twentieth Century.* New York: Harper & Row, 1965.

Picken, Mary Brooks. *The Fashion Dictionary.* New York: Funk & Wagnalls, 1957.

Picken, Mary Brooks and Dora Loues Miller. *Dressmakers of France: The Who, How and Why of French Couture.* New York: Harper & Brothers Publishers, 1956.

Poiret, Paul. *En Habillant l'Epoque.* Paris: Grasset, 1930.

———. *King of Fashion* (autobiography). Translated by Stephen Haden Guest. Philadelphia: J.B. Lippincott Company, 1931.

———. *Revenez-Y.* Paris: Gallemard, 1932.

———. *Art et Finance.* Paris: Lutetia, 1934.

Quant, Mary. *Quant by Quant.* London: Cassell & Co. Ltd., 1966.

Riley, Robert, Dale McConathy, Sally Kirkland, Bernadine Morris, and Eleni Sakes Epstein. *American Fashion: The Life and Lines of Adrian, Mainbocher, McCardell, Norell & Trigère.* Edited by Sarah Tomerlin Lee. New York: Quadrangle/The NY Times Book Co., 1975.

Rochas, Marcel. *Twenty-Five Years of Parisian Elegance, 1925–1950.* Paris: Pierre Tisne, 1951.

Rubin, Leonard G. *The World of Fashion: An Introduction.* New York: Harper & Row Publishers Inc., 1976.

Salomon, Rosalie Kolodny. *Fashion Design for Moderns.* New York: Fairchild Publications, 1976.

Saunders, Edith. *The Age of Worth: Couturier to the Empress Eugénie.* Indiana: Indiana University Press, 1955.

Schiaparelli, Elsa. *Shocking Life.* New York: E.P. Dutton & Co., Inc., 1954.

Snow, Carmel and Mary Louise Aswell. *The World of Carmel Snow.* New York: McGraw-Hill Book Co., 1962.

Spencer, Charles. *Erté.* New York: Clarkson N. Potter, Inc., 1970.

Tolstoy, Mary Koutouzov. *Charlemagne to Dior: The Story of French Fashion.* New York: Michael Slains, 1967.

Vecchio, Walter and Robert Riley. *The Fashion Makers: A Photographic Record.* New York: Crown Publishers, Inc., 1968.

White, Palmer. *Poiret.* New York: Clarkson N. Potter, Inc., 1973.

Williams, Beryl Epstein. *Fashion Is Our Business.* Philadelphia: J.B. Lippincott Co., 1945.

———. *Young Faces in Fashion.* Philadelphia: J.B. Lippincott Co., 1957.

Worth, Jean Philippe. *A Century of Fashion.* Translated by Ruth Scott Miller. Boston: Little, Brown & Co., 1928.

INDEX